# Our Small Stone Cottage in France

Susie Williams

# Our Small Stone Cottage
## in
## France

This edition first published as a Kindle book, May 2015

(First published as 'It's Not Too Late' April 2015)

This paperback edition November 2015

# Also by Susie Williams

# From Goats to a Garden

First published June 2013

Kindle Edition ASIN B00DP6P48O

Paperback Edition ISBN 978-149369444O

# The Flowers in my Bouquet

First published September 2014

Kindle Edition ASIN B00NP457F6

Paperback Edition ISBN978-1502724073

Available from Amazon and other book stores

# Contents

# Acknowledgements

## Information relating to the history of the area

*Mayenne Archives*

*Brecé Ecomusée*

*Les Jardins des Renaudies, Colombiers-du-Plessis*

Most of all, thanks are due to my husband John, for his encouragement and many hours spent organising the photographs, reading and re-reading the text and finalising publication of this book.

# Chapter One
## Well a girl can change her mind you know!

"I'm never coming to France again!" I announced vehemently in October 2010 as we motored north on the A16 for the final few kilometres of our journey towards Calais, the Channel Tunnel and home.

Getting petrol had been a nightmare during this, the most recent of our many holidays in France. We'd been staying in the Dordogne, not far from Bergerac and had become increasingly concerned about the developing fuel crisis. More than a million people had taken to the streets to protest about President Nicolas Sarkozy's pension reforms. France's twelve oil refineries were blocked as part of the protests and hardly any fuel was being distributed. At one time a third of the petrol stations across France were without supplies and with the French half term holiday fast approaching families were worried about their travel plans; there had been panic buying. We were worried too. Would we get home to England?

A few days previously we had visited Hilary, a friend who for several years had been living in the Gers region of south west France. It was some years earlier that she and I had met at French classes in Faversham when we were both living in Kent; she had taken the bold step of moving to France with four generations of her family including her ninety year old mother. This was not our first visit to her French home and although it was a lengthy journey of about three hours each way it was a pleasure to go and visit her and catch up with her news. We said that in some ways we envied her the new life she had made in France; she said to us, 'It's not too late for you to do the same thing you know!'

In the evening on the way back to the Dordogne we came across an automated petrol station that was open for business. Anxious to fill up whenever we could we drove in. One of the pumps was out of action; unfortunately, in manoeuvring to the operational one, my husband, John, pranged the front bumper of the car on a low level obstacle. Oh dear, not a happy moment but at least we had a full tank of fuel again as we set off on our journey north and back to England a few days later. There were some petrol stations open and as we went north we topped up our tank when and where we could. It was a fraught journey.

So there we were at last safely home again in Chichester. As that had definitely been our last French holiday, (or so I thought and said!), I set about looking for destinations in the UK for the following year. We would book four weeks of cottage holidays in different country locations, four cottages that would allow us to take Trixie, our recently acquired rescued greyhound with us.

Now is the time to introduce you to Trixebelle Blue, a sleek gentle five year old bitch who had been a very successful racer at Brighton until earlier in the year when she had been retired. Two years before this our much loved golden lurcher, Tess, had come to the end of her days. We missed having a dog so in the summer of 2010 we went to the Greyhound Rescue Kennels near Brighton and saw many retired greyhounds who were hoping to find a new home now that their racing days were over. And it was there that we found Trixie, a quiet and somewhat nervous dog who was waiting for a new home where she would be loved and understood.

She was very frightened when we brought her home that first day from the Rescue Kennels. The dogs are used to sleeping on low platforms to raise them off the ground; when she went into our house for the first time she saw what she thought could be her sleeping platform. It was where the stairs made a right angle turn after the first two steps making a wider space. That, she thought, was where she would be sleeping. She curled up there looking very miserable. I'm glad to say that she gradually settled in and fortunately took to her new bed in the kitchen, eventually moving to a cosy spot upstairs in my office.

We were soon to learn that she had her foibles, one of which was being determined to stay on track. Well, a good greyhound would, wouldn't it? But now that she was no longer racing, staying on track meant walking on the path through the wood while her owners were manoeuvred into the long wet grass at the side; or cutting a corner in front of you and nearly tripping you up so that she could take the shortest route and get to the winning post first. There was no longer a winning post or a hare on a wire to chase after but cutting corners was in her nature; after five years with us she has not discarded this habit!

We nearly always keep her on her lead in case she races off into the blue distance after a cat, rabbit or small dog and she usually walks very sedately by one's side.

Sometimes she pretends to be a mule, sticking her four legs down solidly as if to say 'I am not walking up that road. There is a white van parked up there and you know I am scared stiff of white vans. In fact I'm scared stiff of quite a lot of things but if you love me I shall get better as time goes on'. She is a lovely gentle dog but does need a lot of care and patience which we are happy to give her.

So several cottage holidays were booked for 2011 and we were looking forward to spending time in the countryside. We had missed it so much since we had left our small holding in Kent three years earlier. I've written about our life there at Larch Cottage, in my book '**From Goats to a Garden**'.

We lived there for nearly thirty years and for the last few years were opening our extensive four acre garden under the National Garden Scheme. But the years moved on and we could see that it wouldn't be long before we would be unable to maintain the garden in the style to which it had become accustomed. It would become a chore and not the pleasure it had been for so many years.

So we moved to Chichester not far from where our younger son lived with his family.

Chichester is an interesting city with its stylish Georgian houses, an impressive cathedral, a famous theatre and a history stretching back to Roman times. As I walked down North Street after parking my car near the Festival Theatre I was struck by the change in our lives from mud and country lanes to broad paved streets and good shopping facilities.

Instead of views over the sweeping lawns and colourful flower beds of Larch Cottage we now had a tiny courtyard garden and were surrounded by houses and streets. However from a back bedroom window there were distant views of the South Downs and after only a fifteen or twenty minute car journey we could be up there enjoying miles of walking on the South Downs Way from which there are views to the north as far as the Hogs Back near Guildford whilst to the south the sea stretches away into the distance. Beautiful.

So there we were in November 2010 enjoying life in Chichester and looking forward to our four country cottage holidays that had been booked for the following year.

I said to John, "What I would really like would be to find a small country cottage of our own that we could pop off to whenever we felt like it rather than having to keep booking other peoples' cottages. Somewhere that is a bit run down, perhaps on the Welsh Borders, so that you could do it up and I could potter in the garden."

"Have a look at property on the Internet and see if there is anything in our price range," was his cautious reply.

Our price range was limited so it was really not very surprising that, especially on the Welsh Borders, property was well above what we could afford. This area is within reach of many highly populated areas like Bristol and

Birmingham, so there is considerable demand.

So I started looking at property in France and despite having stated categorically that I would never go to France again, I was finding details of cottages set in attractive countryside that we could afford. It began to be rather tempting.

The Pas de Calais was quite pricey but that is to be expected as it is within commuting distance of England via the Channel Tunnel. But once I started looking in Lower Normandy prices were very much within our budget.

So we began to build up our criteria.

Firstly, if we bought somewhere it had to be within a day's reach of Chichester via the Channel Tunnel. That took us down as far as the southern part of Normandy, south of Domfront. Secondly we wanted a stone cottage with a wood burner; thirdly a small garden and fourthly we wanted somewhere that was habitable but would give John scope for using his DIY skills. And lastly we wanted somewhere that had long reaching views over the countryside.

There were plenty of memories of the hardships we endured in the first years at Larch Cottage while it was being modernised. We knew we could put up with some discomfort and mess as long as it was all in a good cause. The end result would be our dream cottage. We knew what we were looking for and the search was on.

The end of November is probably not the time of year that normal people would go on a property hunt in France; we are not normal people. The words of my long-time friend Inge come to mind; years ago when she heard of a new project we were embarking on she would exclaim 'You must be mad!' I think maybe we are but I would prefer to think we grasp opportunities. So here we were, planning to do a bit more living and to do it to the full.

\*\*\*\*\*\*\*\*\*\*\*\*\*\*

# Bon Appétit
## Normandy Pork

This is just what we would have chosen to eat when we started our search in November.

Serves four to five people.

1 kg cubed pork, leg or shoulder.

Olive oil

2 onions

Garlic

1 litre Normandy cider

3 eating apples such as Coxes or Braeburn

3-4 Bay leaves

Crème fraiche

Salt and pepper

In a flame proof casserole fry the pork in two to three tablespoons of olive oil until browned on all sides. Set aside. Soften the sliced onions and garlic in the casserole and then put the meat back in to it. If you are not using crème fraiche later you might like to thicken the gravy slightly with a little flour stirred in now. Add seasoning and cover with some Normandy cider and bring to the boil, stirring. Place thick slices of peeled and cored eating apple on top of the meat. Add three or four bay leaves to add to the flavour and enhance the cooking aromas. Cook at 160°C fan oven for two hours. Then stir in some crème fraiche if you like a creamy sauce. A French dish like this deserves French bread to mop up the delicious juices. And of course more of that tasty Normandy cider to drink with it.

\*\*\*\*\*\*\*

# Chapter Two
## The Search is On

During our earlier holiday in the Dordogne Trixie had gone into kennels. We had been advised that she would be fine as she had lived in kennels for all of her life but in fact she wasn't. She had just begun to settle in after being with us for about four months and there we were, from her point of view, turfing her out again. Poor dog.

We found out on our return from France that she had been unwell, so we decided that we would not leave her in kennels again. When we went to France to look for 'our cottage' it was time once more to call in our trusty home sitter.

John Tomblin had often stayed at Larch Cottage looking after things when we went away. We used to say the place looked better when we came home than it had before we went. He was marvellous. He watered the pots and kept the colourful displays in them at their best; he watered the garden if necessary; he kept an eye on plants in the green houses; he dead headed the roses and so the list went on. But above all he looked after our golden lurcher Tess and took her for long walks through the woods and orchards among which we lived. He was a country person at heart and very much enjoyed coming to us. Sometimes his wife Cathy came as well and she joined in with dead heading any flowers past their best and generally keeping an eye on John. He also came once or twice to look after Tess after we had moved to Chichester, but she was about fifteen then and died the following year.

We needed someone to look after Trixie while we went cottage hunting in France. We turned again to John Tomblin. "I hoped you would ask me," was his response. While we were away he coped with her foibles such as when she was in a mulish mood and refused to walk up the road with him. He summed her up in a very few words. "She's a madam and a half".

So on a gloomy day at the end of November

2010 as soon as he had arrived to take over the reins we set off for the two hour drive to Folkestone and the Channel Tunnel. Once we were in France I took over the wheel in order to give John a break after driving on the busy English roads. We had decided to go via Caen and the Suisse Normande to keep our appointment the next day with an estate agent at Passais-La-Conception where we had located a barn that sounded as if it might be just what we were looking for.

It was a miserable late autumn day for a journey and as we turned onto the A13 towards Caen it started to get dark and it was raining heavily.

'Oh dear', we said.

'Are we foolish to be setting out on this venture?'

'Should we just go home again tomorrow and forget all about it?'

It didn't get any better when the hoped for meal at a service area near Caen did not materialise ('Restaurant closed for renovations') and neither could we find anywhere else to eat. We drove in the dark through the Suisse Normande and as expected it was hilly, the roads twisted and turned through the black night, there were no views to encourage us on our way and there were patches of drifting fog. It was not an easy journey. Our venture had not got off to a good start.

We had booked into a bed and breakfast place at Passais but the owners were away that evening and a friend of theirs let us in; for a meal we had to make do with the remnants of our picnic. The room was comfortable and we had a good night so with our spirits buoyed up again next morning we set off in yet more rain to keep our appointment with Margareta, the estate agent.

We met her in the village square in front of the church and followed in our car as she led the way to the nearby barn. The photo of the barn on the Internet looked encouraging. There appeared to be a new roof and the information led us to believe that at least some of the building would be habitable. There was about a third of an acre of rough grass which could be made into a garden. But what we saw when we arrived was that the roof was only partly done and the inside needed a complete rebuild. Rain was streaming in through holes in the unfinished roof, soaking the lower walls and earthen floors. There was no ceiling, there were no stairs, and indeed, no intact upper floor whatsoever. This wouldn't do at all. Plans had been drawn up for the completion of the building which finally would have five bedrooms and would probably cost in excess of £75,000 to complete. In no way could it be lived in whilst carrying out the work and that work would take many months. We didn't have that sort of money to spend and in any case we didn't want a property of that size.

So what to do next? Go home and forget the whole idea perhaps? Certainly not! Margareta had a plan. She suggested that she should take us a further eleven miles south to the town of Gorron where her friend Barbara was an 'Immobilier' and had many properties on her books. So that is what we did and within a short time we had been introduced to the charming

Barbara who spoke very good English. We sat in her office in Gorron where a short list of four suitable properties was drawn up.

In drawing up this list we reiterated our criteria; a stone cottage with a wood burner, partially habitable and with scope for John to use his DIY skills for renovation. It must have good views over the surrounding countryside. Oh yes and a small garden.

One or two phone calls were made making appointments to view these properties and then we set off with Margareta to see the first one. It was empty as its English owners had already gone back to England so we were able go straight there.

*We see the cottage and its garden for the first time*

The cottage was near to the village of Brecé, which is about two miles from Gorron. We turned into a single track lane and then onto a driveway which served a cluster of cottages. The garden ran alongside the lane but was badly neglected with dense mounds of blackberry briers and some overgrown trees but it was level and a good size.

We went inside; downstairs there was one good sized room which served as kitchen, dining room and sitting room. It had a tiled floor, a beamed ceiling and the all-important wood burner. There was also a downstairs loo near the foot of the rather steep stairs which led up to what once would have been the hay loft. There were two tiny bedrooms, one of which was full of sundry items, and a shower room with another loo. My goodness two loos in a tiny cottage! That was luxury.

All the lower walls upstairs had exposed stonework and untreated beams of sawn timber, with plywood nailed to them, creating a ceiling. None of these rooms had been finished but had got to the stage of being divided up with greyish plasterboard. The installation of the electricity upstairs had not been finished either and stray cables trailed over and down the walls like exotic creepers. The shower room and part of the landing did not have the benefit of any ceiling, we looked up to the underside of the roof slates and festoons of dusty cobwebs. It was quite a mess but John felt that he could cope with the necessary work. We knew it would have to be professionally re-wired.

We went down stairs again and out into the garden and there was the last of our criteria, the view. It overlooked a tree lined valley and extended into the distance over farmland and finally to wooded hills in the distance. The valley turned out to be very special but we didn't discover how special until the following year.

*Brecé village in the distance*

So this little cottage at La Vesquerie had ticked all the boxes and there was no point in looking any further. It was quite clear that this was going to be 'our' French cottage and as for never going to France again, as I had so categorically stated only a month earlier, it was now clear that we were going to spend a great deal of time in France.

So it was back into Gorron with Margareta. Since it was now lunch time and the Immobilier was closed we went to have lunch at a nearby bistro; then to Barbara to declare our interest in the property. We gave her our mobile phone number and asked her to contact the vendors with our offer hoping she would be able to phone us back before the afternoon was over.

We went back to view La Vesquerie just from the outside this time and venture further down the single track lane to see what lay beyond the cottage. The lane sloped gently down through fields towards the valley, terminating at a tumble-down place called La Closerie. The rain had stopped and late afternoon autumn sunshine bathed the valley as we turned the car round and went back to the cottage where we waited hoping for the phone call. Had we known what lay further down the hill beyond La Closerie we would have been even more excited. That had to wait for the next time we came to see La Vesquerie but that was to be months ahead.

We'd been sitting in the drive for only a few minutes when the phone call came. Our offer had been accepted! So it was back to Barbara's office feeling very excited to find out what the next stage in acquiring our French cottage would be and then home to England where we would need to set up a bank account in France and arrange for the transfer of funds for the deposit. Suddenly there was a whole new range of things to learn about and do!

A few days later we went to see our son and daughter-in-law. As we went in carrying the file with all the cottage information in it Sue eyed it and said, "You're not moving are you?"

I think she had always been worried that the Chichester house with its tiny garden would not satisfy us after the four acres of Larch Cottage. In fact as things turned out it could not have been more ideal. Anyway there we were announcing that we were buying a cottage in France. I think they were quite surprised at this unexpected development! However, they quickly caught our enthusiasm and were very interested in how it would all work out.

\*\*\*\*\*\*\*\*\*\*\*\*\*\*

*Immobiliére in Gorron*

# Bon Appétit
## An Omelette

Into an omelette pan put a little olive oil and set it on a high heat.

While it is heating up whisk two large eggs with three tablespoons of water, salt and pepper.

When the pan is hot pour in the egg mixture. It should sizzle nicely. Draw the mixture gently towards the centre and tilt the pan so that the uncooked egg can slide under the outer edges. When it is golden underneath but still slightly runny on the top turn the omelette onto a warm plate. Simple and delicious.

A piece of crusty baguette and a green salad are perfect with this. And a glass of southern Rhone red wine such as Vacqueyras.

*******

# Chapter Three
## We Become the Owners of a Cottage in France

We had plenty to think about during the winter as we made plans for what we would do to the cottage. On the spare room bed the pile of things to take there on our next visit had been growing. It was an exciting time looking forward to our new venture and it certainly livened up the gloomy winter days.

But first we had to take steps to obtain Trixie's pet passport. That involved getting her immunised against rabies and then waiting for the required six months for it to become valid. Within two years the regulations had changed and a much shorter time is now required for pet passports to become valid after the rabies immunisation. But then it was six months, so we knew we wouldn't be able to take her to France until the beginning of June 2011.

Finally in February 2011 we received

notification from Barbara that all the necessary checks and legal requirements had been completed and we could make plans to go and meet the Notaire in her office and sign the documents and complete the purchase. So again we arranged for John Tomblin to come and look after Trixie and this time it was to be for five days, one day each way for the journey and three days there. It was very exciting.

We had collected a great many items to take with us. John had put together an 'essential tool kit', which would remain at the cottage. Various items of furniture had been recovered from the loft space in Chichester, and there were work clothes including heavy duty overalls as we knew we were going to be dealing with dust and plasterboard in abundance.

Our car was loaded up to the roof, packed so fully that nothing moved out of place during the 400 mile road journey. Thankfully, this journey was much less stressful than the previous visit in November, though it took a little longer than anticipated; we did not reach the B & B in Brecé until about 9pm, but were warmly welcomed and shared a much needed hot meal with the owners, who had waited for us. The following morning, feeling very excited, we went off to finalise the purchase of La Vesquerie, buying some vital food supplies at the local Super U en route.

We met Barbara, the Notaire and our agent in Gorron, and the signing began. Not a quick event! Every page of the sale details had to be read to us, unfamiliar phrases clarified, and I had to sign all the documents with my maiden name; after being married for forty-five years that was a bit odd. Each one of some sixty pages had to be either signed or initialled by both of us. Finally, the Notaire was satisfied, all monies had changed hands, and we had the key!

We were all set to get going. But first Margareta took on a battle with the local water people to get our supply officially turned on. We would never have managed without her determined negotiations as our French was just not up to it. Earlier, John had spent many hours (so it seemed to him) arranging for the electricity account to be set up in our name. And before that, setting up a bank account in France had not been simple; however, success eventually, and we went to the local branch in Gorron to collect a cheque book and debit card, which were essential.

At last there we were opening the door of our own French cottage! It seemed strange going in again after so many months absence. We wondered if we would still like it and what condition it would be in. Although we had taken some photos on our first visit we couldn't remember all the details of its interior.

The first job was to open the two sets of shutters downstairs and let in some light. It was much as we remembered it and the fearful festoons of loose cables on the landing again filled us with disquiet.

*Photo on the next page*

*The Landing*

There were the two tiny bedrooms which we had already decided were going to become one larger one, and the rather grim shower room. The partially finished ceilings to the landing and shower room had some old carpet covering the gaps overhead. It was all rather basic but we were undaunted as we already knew there was plenty of work to be done.

We were impressed with the way the previous owners had cleared everything out and left the place as clean as possible; we had been anxious they might have left all the discarded items behind. But no, it had all gone apart from a few items of furniture that we had agreed to buy from them.

After a quick look round it was time to unload the car. John unpacked the large quantity of tools that he would need and also there were sheets, duvets, pillows, towels, crockery, cutlery, saucepans, electric kettle, table lamps, an extra heater, a television and some warm winter clothes for us. We had brought an oak storage chest that would eventually hold sheets and towels on the landing and of course this was fully packed for the journey plus two bedside cupboards also full of items.

In Gorron there was at that time an English bed shop in Rue Magenta and we had been able to arrange that two single beds would be delivered to the cottage later that afternoon. It had been pointed out to us that French beds were often shorter than English beds and once we started to live there we realised that indeed the local Normans were generally a bit shorter than many English people. About my height in fact and rounded, like me too. In fact if you saw tall, well-built and especially blond people you could be fairly sure they were not local to

Gorron. It made me wonder what William the Conqueror's Norman soldiers looked like as they fought their way up the hill at Battle in 1066.

The short February day was moving rapidly on and with the beds coming later that afternoon we started to sort out our possessions. I began to get the kitchen organised and put the shopping away. There were plenty of cupboards to put our things in and there was the fridge we had bought from the previous owners and also a gas cooker. We had also bought the cane furniture and a dining table and chairs that they had used so downstairs started to look reasonably homely especially when John had managed to get the wood burner alight. That gave out a good amount of heat and with rushing around getting sorted out we didn't feel particularly cold. There were two oil filled electric heaters as well, one of which was used upstairs.

Much to our relief the beds and mattresses arrived on time, in kit form, and were put together for us. It was a relief to know that we

*Beds to sleep in!*

would have somewhere warm and comfortable to sleep and I quickly made them up with the sheets, pillows and duvets and switched on the electric blankets. Life was beginning to look a bit more civilised.

One member of the team that put the beds together was Jack, son of Stuart who did gardening and garden clearing. We were only too pleased to get to know Stuart who, with his wife Carol, cut the grass for us in the first year. It was arranged that they would come and clear the huge mounds of brambles from the garden and eventually, before we came back with Trixie in June, put up a secure fence to keep her within bounds.

Meanwhile John had made a start on demolishing part of the stud wall that divided the two small bedrooms. By the next day it was all down and we had one large bedroom. But all was chaos. His workbench occupied the far end of the room and insulation material that had been between the two layers of plasterboard was piled up on one side as was the wood and plasterboard to be re-used. The general effect was like being in a cardboard box as the plaster board was a grey-brown colour. At the end of the bedroom by our bedheads the wall was dingy and mildewed. What a good thing it is that the initial enthusiasm helps you to overcome these hardships. I remember it was just the same at Larch Cottage in the early days.

It was dark and cold when we woke up the next morning but soon the fire was alight and the shutters open letting in daylight. We were eager to use to the full the remainder of our short time there and to make the cottage seem like home as soon as possible.

*The enlarged bedroom*

John got to work repositioning the doorways to the bedroom and shower room and then went off to buy two new doors. In France you buy the doors complete with frames round them; as long as the space they are to occupy is correct, fitting them should not be too much of a problem.

Having the place re-wired was a priority and Rob, an English electrician living in France, came to see us the next day. It was arranged that before we came again in March he would rewire upstairs and fit two electrically heated towel rails, one in the shower room and one in the down stairs loo. I remember him remarking that at least we had a fuse box so it would be safe for us to use the electricity for the time being.

We also had a satellite dish fitted so that we were able to receive English television programmes, not that we had much time to spend watching television. I think it was then that we were told that you could distinguish which houses were lived in by English people by whether or not they had satellite dishes on their roofs. I'm not sure that is always the case.

With all the dust around we needed some fresh air and allowed ourselves a bit of time off to walk down the lane to La Closerie which we had seen on our very first visit in the previous November.

We were keen to explore and see what lay round the corner. At La Closerie there were two tumble down cottages and the remains of what must once have been an orchard and a vegetable garden. To the left of this dereliction

*Ruined cottage at La Closerie*

was a track and we followed it round the side of the building and down a slope.

At the bottom we were amazed to find a river and an old mill. A narrow footbridge led to the other side of the river. This was the River Colmont which rises several miles to the north near Le Teilleul and, fed by numerous streams that drain the farmland, gradually makes its way south to join first of all the River Mayenne and then the mighty River Loire. Several months later we set out to explore the source of the River Colmont. We found it in a marshy field where first it became a trickle and then a stream and then a few miles further on a small river with meanders and a distinct flood plain. Further downstream, between Gorron and Mayenne, the river enters a gorge-like section where it tumbles and rushes noisily over rocks and rapids and is our favourite walking area, only a few hundred yards from the cottage.

But on that first day when we explored beyond La Closerie we crossed over and found a path that ran alongside the river and then through the water meadows further on. Later there would be wood anemones and bluebells but this was still February, the trees were leafless and it was wet and muddy underfoot. We discovered that this path was one of a network of paths that ran near the river for several miles and this particular path was part of a circuit that started in Brecé, came up through the fields,

*Looking upstream from the bridge*

past our cottage and down to the river again.

Brecé Mill is one of three old mills in this part of the valley and ancient footpaths go through the woods to them just above the flood plain. I can imagine farmers hundreds of years ago making their way to the mills with a sack of grain on their backs or on a donkey if they were lucky enough to own one.

We were delighted to find these footpaths and the marked walks. It made us feel that in finding La Vesquerie we had been incredibly fortunate as walking with the dog was a part of our daily lives and something we enjoyed doing very much.

The countryside around La Vesquerie is 'bocage' landscape with small fields separated by earthen banks topped with trees and many wild flowering plants. There are hidden sunken lanes. This is the Mayenne area of the Pays de la Loire just south of the Normandy region.

Our short visit ended all too quickly and we were off back to England until the next trip to the cottage in March. Once more, John Tomblin came to look after Trixie and the house; it was exciting to think that on our next visit in June we should be taking Trixie with us.

We couldn't wait to get back and when we arrived just as dusk was falling there was a hint of spring in the air and one solitary daffodil was blooming in the garden. It was wonderful to see that Rob had been busy and there were no longer loose cables upstairs and that we had the luxury of heated towel rails in the downstairs loo and the shower room which warmed those rooms too. And, with a proper fuse box installed we were safe. It had been a shock to us when he had sent us an email a week or two after our first visit saying he'd opened up the old fuse box and found that the wires poked through the holes in the box were not actually connected to the main supply. So during our brief stay there in February we had been in the rather dangerous situation of using electricity straight from the main supply.

Again we had only three days at the cottage; we had to get moving. John's priority was to get proper ceilings fixed on the landing and in the shower room so that we were hopefully cut off from the spiders and mice in the loft.

I put fresh white paint on the wall by the head of our beds and thus covered up the dinginess that had been there before. Things were getting very much better.

Outside I raked together the dead brambles that Stuart had cut down and had a huge bonfire. This gave me a chance to look at the garden and to start looking forward to what we would be able to do to make it more attractive. At Larch Cottage after our sheep and goat keeping days were over we'd used the four acres there to make a varied and interesting garden which we opened to the public for charity so I couldn't wait to get started on this new garden. I'm not keen on straight lines in a garden and prefer curves but with the remains of a path running alongside what may once have been a flower border adjacent to the tall Thuja plicata hedge, it seemed we would have to go with that for the time being. But there wasn't enough time to get started on this visit. That would have to wait until we came again in June.

Again at the end of our short visit we had to tear ourselves away but cheered ourselves up with the thought that next time we would be bringing Trixie and would be able to stay for five weeks.

Looking back we're not quite sure when we made the transition from thinking of La Vesquerie as a holiday home that we would go to for a couple of weeks now and then, to a place where we would spend up to six months of the year. All of our working lives and beyond we'd gone away for two weeks once or twice a year.

When we were first married it had been camping in a home conversion of a Ford van, then when I went back to teaching after having the children we bought a frame tent and went camping in style. Much later we went off in our caravan and later still, as we got older went for the luxury of holiday cottages.

We had spent many holidays in different parts of Britain, above all in Pembrokeshire near St David's, but in later years we had taken our caravan to various parts of France where one of our favourite places was near the Alpine village of Vallouise near Briançon which I had first visited as a school girl in 1956. We'd also explored Spain extensively by car and had several wonderful holidays in that beautiful, mountainous country, visiting Granada where we stayed in the Parador overlooking the Alhambra, also Cáceres, Seville and Cordoba and spent a week in an isolated cortijo high up in the Sierra Nevada south of Granada.

To celebrate my fiftieth birthday we'd done our own version of a Grand Tour by car, going to Italy by motor rail, then taking in Pisa, Florence and Venice before driving through Austria to Salzburg and returning through the Black Forest in Germany. We'd been to the Italian Lakes as well, so although we hadn't been to exotic places on the other side of the world we'd had some wonderful holidays and seen a wide variety of scenery.

But now here we were with our own holiday home in France and quite frankly the desire to travel long distances had left us. We were very content to be in our own place which has become more like home the longer we are here.

Eventually when the cottage renovations would be finished and the garden looking wonderful we could think of nothing more appealing than to sit in our garden looking at the fabulous view spread out before us over the valley and into the tree covered distance. Two years of hard and messy work were ahead of us though before we could get to that stage but most days we both got out in the afternoon to take Trixie for her walk and explore a little more of the surrounding countryside.

\*\*\*\*\*\*\*\*\*\*\*\*\*

# Bon Appétit
## Poires au Vin Rouge

Here is an opportunity to make use of the plentiful supply of Normandy pears in the autumn.

6 dessert pears

A bottle of red wine.

A piece of cinnamon stick

150g sugar

Place the wine, sugar and cinnamon stick in a large saucepan and heat gently until the sugar is dissolved. Boil for five minutes. Peel the pears leaving the stalk on and add them to the syrup in the pan. Cover and simmer gently for thirty minutes turning them if necessary so they are immersed in the liquid. Leave in the liquid to cool. Enjoy.

*******

# Chapter Four
## Trixie goes to France

So at last June arrived, Trixie's passport was now valid and she could join us on our trips to France. She is a good traveller and settled down to sleep on the dog shelf in the back of the car, which as usual was packed with a huge amount of luggage.

Actually sleeping is what greyhounds do best, so that worked out well. Nevertheless the cottage was another new place for her to get used to and she was a bit subdued for the first day or so. Stuart had securely fenced the whole garden so she could be let out there without any danger of her escaping. Before long she was enjoying racing round the garden at great speed and we began to get an idea of what she must have looked like on the race track at Brighton. As her confidence increased, we were amused to observe that she created different circuits within the space available; sometimes it was the entire perimeter, or it might be a short course with tight turns, or a figure of eight around the potager that was created later in the year.

In our tiny garden in Chichester there is no scope for her to run and when taking her for walks we always keep on her lead in case she runs off after a rabbit, cat or small dog. But here when cyclists and runners go past she gets quite excited and likes to show them that she can move faster than they can.

I enjoy taking her down the lane first thing in the morning when the world is fresh and dewy and so very quiet. Sometimes we see deer making their way to the river and I have to hold tightly on to her lead as there is nothing she would like better than to chase them. I have heard that a greyhound can bring a deer down and I would hate that to happen.

The peace here is remarkable, sometimes there is just total silence, sometimes there is a profusion of bird song and since it is a busy agricultural area a tractor can often be heard somewhere during the working day. Indeed at haymaking and harvesting time the hardworking farmers are often seen and heard still working as it gets dark.

But generally it is very quiet and that is particularly noticeable at lunch time. At midday the traffic ceases on the distant main road and the car park in the village is full of lorries and trucks as their drivers enjoy a proper meal at Le Briccius, the restaurant in the village. A three course lunch with coffee is offered for the modest price of 12€. On the tables there is a bottle of red wine, a bottle of cider and a bottle of water.

We go there to eat sometimes and it's good to see the workers enjoying their midday break. There is no rowdyism and no over indulgence of the freely available alcohol. And the food, although not haute cuisine, is extremely good and varied. But I must make a small mention about ladies wanting to visit the loo and say it's probably best avoided when the workmen have just come in as first you have to brush past them lined up at the urinals as you make your way to the cubicle at the end. This is France!

So here we were at the beginning of five long weeks at our cottage in France. What a wonderful opportunity this was to press on with the renovation. Tempting though it was in some ways to explore our surroundings and settle in to French life, to us it was more important to turn the cottage into home as quickly as possible and to enjoy living in a comfortable environment.

Unfortunately, the previous owners of the cottage who had bought it twenty years earlier had only been able to be there for short periods of time; they had never been able to achieve their goal of fully modernising the place. They had done a lot of work downstairs, had tiled the floor, panelled the walls, painted the beams, fitted out the downstairs loo and had a new 'fosse septique' installed. They had added stairs, albeit extremely steep ones, and upstairs had put in a loo, basin and shower and lined most of the walls with plasterboard. They had divided the space into two tiny bedrooms and fitted Velux windows. But after twenty years it still wasn't finished so I think it must have been rather disheartening. I imagine when they came it was all work and who wants to spend all their holidays working? So in the end they decided to sell and the cottage was perfect for us, habitable but with some work left to do.

Our younger son and family were keen to see what we had bought before we had done much to it, but parts of it were so awful that we had to make some improvements in the two weeks before they arrived. John had managed to get the ceilings finished upstairs so we were no longer exposed to the mice and spiders in the loft space, but the shower room looked pretty grim with unpainted walls, exposed stone and pipework and aged blue carpet tiles scattered on the floor. The first job was to paint the plasterboard walls and ceiling white and to replace the carpet tiles with a carpet remnant from our home in Chichester. The exposed pipes and stonework would have to wait until later. Anyway after that work was done it looked quite a lot better.

Originally the cottage had a low doorway at the front; it had a ladder going up to the former hay loft that would have been used as a storage area, with no ceiling, just the rafters and slates above. By the time we arrived the ladder had gone and steep stairs had been installed elsewhere. Downstairs had become one room. The ladder space had been filled in with a pine box like construction; more will be said about that later.

I think one of the things that had worried me most during the winter of 2010/2011, was the steepness of those stairs. We weren't as young and agile as we used to be and I felt that the stairs were dangerous. So fixing those was a priority job as well as putting a balustrade along the landing so we wouldn't fall off the edge. John could see that by putting a turn at the top of the stairs he would be able to reduce their steepness. This involved much mysterious engineering to remove a floor beam and provide additional support for a new quarter landing with just two further stairs to the first floor. When this was done it turned out to be 'Stairs Mark Two' and the old stairs were reused in a slightly different configuration. Later would come the final version but 'Stairs Mark Two' was a big improvement for the time being.

*The quarter turn*

*The landing*

Our visitors duly arrived and were keen to see what we had taken on. Later we took them down to the river but unfortunately it was pouring with rain so they didn't see it at its best.

Our son had brought his chain saw and set to work cutting down an old elder tree near the cottage that did not add anything to the planned attractiveness of the garden.

In the following days John removed the rest of the tree and took his sledge hammer to a strange and rather ugly concrete bench that had been underneath it. It was odd to think that other people long ago had sat there, perhaps admiring the wonderful view. But that part of the garden had over the years become completely overgrown with ivy and needed clearing.

The time had now come when, as John worked inside, I could make a serious start on the garden. So initially I started clearing what came to be known as the 'Long Border'. I think previously it must have been known as 'The Dump' because no one in the past had any thoughts of making it an attractive border and as it was almost adjacent to the cottage it was the obvious place to dump rubbish. So I started digging and the first thing I noticed was the amount of thin branches and grass cuttings that had been dumped there over the years. The organic matter was dug in and the branches removed to the end of the garden for another bonfire.

Well, I say the end of the garden but where exactly was the end of the garden? Many years

before someone had planted a box hedge there but it had never been cut, so now it was twenty feet high as were some bay trees also planted long ago. Our neighbour's small orchard was beyond that but due to the height of the overgrown and neglected greenery his plum trees had grown tall and spindly. The inevitable ivy had twined itself round everything and it was impossible to see where our land ended.

So as a break from clearing the border-to-be I started hacking away at this jungle. After a while I found we could gain about eight feet of ground by going right back to our boundary. The more I cleared the higher the bonfire mound became.

*The old privy*

A great surprise awaited me as I cut my way into the far corner nearest to our neighbour's land, for there was the original privy with its door hanging off, constructed from oak planks presumably made from locally grown trees goodness knows how many years ago; a hundred, two hundred perhaps? I guess it was last used by the people who lived here maybe thirty years ago.

The previous owners of the cottage had sent us a photograph of the garden that clearly showed a gravel path they'd had laid alongside the border; now, apart from a depression in the ground, there was no gravel to be seen for it had become overgrown with weeds. I set myself the task of clearing that as well. Never having used a pick axe before I found the task very heavy going and only managed to clear a few inches a day. But eventually it was done. Some months later we had fresh gravel put on the top and it made a good path alongside which I planted lavender which grew quickly to make an attractive edge.

*Progress!*

And I continued to clear the border. One of my plans included having somewhere to grow vegetables and salads, so although it wasn't the final location for our 'potager', for the first summer I decided to grow tomatoes, beetroot and peas at the end of the border. Trixie was keenly observing all this digging and decided that as it was such a good game she would join in as well. I would come out in the morning to find she'd dug what she thought was a really useful hole. I did not share her view so we decided to fix a low wire fence at the front of the border. This was not ideal and even less so when much later I tripped over it and landed on the gravel path and ended up with grazed and bloody knees like a six year old in the school playground.

The clearing went on and various items emerged, the most interesting being the original shallow white sink from the cottage.

This discovery filled me with ideas of restoring the kitchen to its original form and going all rustic and distressed. John was horrified but as usual when I have crazy ideas he mostly holds his tongue and waits for me to grow out of it which fortunately in this case I did.

Although we had at first planned to completely finish decorating upstairs before doing anything else, downstairs the kitchen was becoming a problem. Some units had been placed across the window; in order to open it you had to climb up and over them, not ideal when you are approaching seventy or indeed any other time. The small fridge wasn't large enough, the gas oven didn't work at all and the gas burners on the hob were very temperamental. It wasn't a kitchen that I was happy working in. So the task of modernising and reorganising it became part of the plan for our next visit. We had already decided that the units across the window would have to be moved immediately. The new washing machine went in a line adjacent to the sink and the remaining cupboards made a peninsular unit forming a room divider between the kitchen and sitting room area. At last there was easy access to the window.

In the meantime John felt it was essential to establish the location of the fosse septique. This had been installed by the previous owners but it was not clear exactly where it was and there were no inspection points. So making what he hoped was a reasoned guess at its location by the unevenness of the lawn, he started digging. 'Oh great' Trixie thought now that she couldn't access the flower-bed-to be, 'Maybe I'm allowed to join in!'

But by the time he'd gone down some way I think even she felt it was a hole too far so she stood by it in a supervisory role as he dug deeper. Down and down he went, ever widening his scope but eventually, eureka! There was the drain leading into the tank.

When we lived on our small holding in Kent we became used to dealing with a septic tank so this was familiar to us. Obviously it was necessary to raise the inspection traps to ground level to be accessible for when it need emptying. More hard work for poor John and much more back ache but eventually it was done. And three years later we were very thankful that we had done this work.

So that area was dealt with for the time being. Prior to our arrival the inspector of drains had noted that the kitchen drain merely led into a soak away and needed connecting to the drain into the fosse. We noticed with some concern that all the water from the washing machine and the kitchen sink was overflowing and making a river down the drive we shared with our next door neighbour so eventually more excavations would have to be done but they had to wait for a while.

We were coming to the end of our five week stay at the cottage but one last job before we went back to England was to get the wardrobe fitted out. John always needs plenty of storage, not particularly for clothes but for electrical things like plugs, cables, spare fuses and light bulbs, tools and 'things that might come in useful one day' and that surprisingly often do.

So in setting up the wardrobe he was able to recycle a set of drawers from the kitchen reorganisation. That gave good storage space for tools and the rest of the cupboard was fitted out with a hanging rail and two shelves. Doors however were not essential and they had to wait until considerably later.

So that really was the end of our first long stay at the cottage and we went home for about three weeks at the beginning of July. A lot had been accomplished but a lot remained to be done and it had been decided that the kitchen would be the first priority when we came back.

\*\*\*\*\*\*\*\*\*\*\*\*\*\*

# Bon Appétit
## Quiche Lorraine

Ready rolled shortcrust pastry

200g lardons and three large eggs

200ml crème fraiche

200ml double cream

Pepper, salt and grated nutmeg

50g Gruyère cheese

Quiche Lorraine is delicious hot or cold. I do have a preference for the small individual ones which are good for picnics but you might prefer a larger one for serving at table. I use ready rolled pastry from Super U as it saves a lot of time that I would rather spend in the garden. Line a large fluted quiche tin or six small ones with shortcrust pastry. Line the pastry cases with foil, shiny side down and fill with beans. Bake at 200°C in a fan oven for ten to fifteen minutes. Remove foil and beans. Brush the pastry with beaten egg and return to the oven for five minutes. Meanwhile fry the lardons until slightly browned. Drain on kitchen paper. Whisk the eggs, with the crème fraiche and the double cream, a pinch of salt, a grind of black pepper and a small amount of freshly grated nutmeg. This is very rich so milk could be substituted for the cream if you wish. Cut 30g of the cheese into small dice. Grate the rest. Put the lardons and diced cheese in the base of the pastry case and carefully pour in the cream mixture. Sprinkle the grated cheese on the top. Cook at 190°C for about twenty-five minutes or twenty minutes for the small quiches. Ideal eaten warm or cold with a green salad freshly picked from the garden. For a vegetarian version substitute cooked and sliced mushrooms for the lardons.

I have found with the small quiches that it is not necessary to bake them blind providing they go onto a preheated baking tray in the oven set at 200°C. I have also used milk instead of any cream or crème fraiche but I did put extra grated cheese on the top.

*******

# Chapter Five
## On with the jobs

It is possible that had we been doing the kitchen a couple of years later we would have known exactly where to buy what we wanted in France but back then, although we were making a good start on getting to know where the various bricolage (do-it-yourself) stores were, we felt more confident that we would get exactly what we wanted by buying in England. So while we were at home we bought a gas hob and stainless steel sink. Yes, much to John's relief, I had got over the idea of using the damaged white porcelain one I had dug up in the garden.

It is quite unnecessary to bring most goods from the UK. Apart from the bother of transporting bulky items there are likely to be small but decisive differences in connection fittings, and repairs or guarantee work may be almost impossible.

One of John's Christmas presents had been a book of French Building terms, and this was invaluable. Sometimes there were language difficulties at the builders' yard which John overcame by using his phone to photograph the item he was looking for and showing this to the yard man if all else failed; it proved to be a very successful system.

So there we were fully loaded up again as we set off on 27th July for the Channel Tunnel and France with Trixie on the dog shelf as usual at the back of the car.

It was good to be back at the cottage. Stuart and Carol had been to cut the grass and strim the bank at the side of the lane, the border was looking better than it had last time we arrived and now we were ready to get on with the kitchen. We'd located some cupboards we liked at Ikea so leaving Trixie to look after the cottage we made the three hour round trip to Rennes and came back loaded up with our new cupboards and fittings for them. A work surface bought locally was delivered and then we were ready to go.

At the same time Robert Cannon came to line the stone walls in the bedroom and on the landing upstairs. We had spent some time discussing what we were going to do with them. Should they be repointed and left as bare stone? Should they just be painted white? Or should they be lined with insulation and plaster board? We opted for the latter as the walls were in a bad condition and we felt insulating and lining them would be the neatest and warmest option.

*Covering and insulating the wall*

*The bedroom completed*

Now a few years later I think we undoubtedly made the right choice. We had sealed out the spiders and other creepy crawlies and sealed in the heat in cold weather. Robert made a splendid job of this and topped it off with stout oak shelves. There is an abundance of oak in France, it is readily available at sensible prices, and is well seasoned. We were very pleased with the result and I was glad that John had agreed to have the work done as he had a huge amount to do anyway.

So there we were, utter chaos upstairs and down, John working on the kitchen downstairs at the same time as Robert with his assistant Leo was working upstairs but the end result was very well worthwhile. Apart that is, from poor John's backache. He was shifting a lot of heavy stuff around but the kitchen work surface was the heaviest of all.

*Work begins on the kitchen*

After a few days we had a new electric cooker and a new gas hob; we'd bought a larger fridge and had good cupboards with wire drawers that slid in and out for ease of access. And we had a new washing machine which had to come in through the window because the doorway was too narrow. When it arrived the delivery men announced that it was 'blessé' (wounded) and would we still accept it if twenty euros was knocked off the price? Well a slight scratch on one side where it didn't show anyway and twenty euros knocked off the price seemed a good deal to us so we had no problem in welcoming it through the window and into the kitchen. After all John's hard work I was very pleased with my new kitchen.

After Robert had finished his work upstairs we painted the bedroom and landing in fresh white paint and had a serviceable grey carpet fitted with enough left over to do the stairs in the autumn.

And then just after John's birthday and our wedding anniversary in August it was time to go home for our annual family week end.

We were back at the cottage by the beginning of September ready for a final push with jobs before we came back home for the long winter months. Work remained to be done in the kitchen as we worked out where to put the wall cupboards. I remember that one of them had three locations before we finally decided to abandon wall cupboards altogether.

However the downstairs walls were still a mixture of pale mud colour on some walls and primrose yellow on others. With the dark beams above our heads and the ginger colour of the pine wall panelling in the sitting area we were keen to paint everywhere fresh white to maximise the light. However there wouldn't be time to get that done this year.

Also during that September John completed the shower room by fitting a new loo and basin with work surface beside it and cupboards underneath. He built a cupboard round the small water tank and completely enclosed all the pipe work and the cistern.

What an improvement! There was enough of
the grey carpet that had been fitted in the

bedroom to put in there and it looked good.

We had a week's holiday booked in the Dordogne for October but a week or so before we were due to go John had the misfortune to fall down the stairs. He'd been suffering from back ache again with all the heavy work he'd been doing and had gone upstairs to lie flat on the bed for a while to see if it would help. Unfortunately as he came down stairs he slipped on one of the narrow treads and fell heavily down the last three or four stairs. Well it could have been a lot worse; bones could have been broken but as it was he was in great pain and had the most horrific bruising. (*Photo not allowed as this is a family book*).

These were Stairs Mark Two you may remember, which were a modification of the stairs that were here when we bought the cottage. They really were a compromise with the treads being too narrow. So the accident prompted the installation of Stairs Mark Three which were the final and completely satisfactory version.

John felt he would be too uncomfortable

sitting in the car for the six or seven hour journey to the Dordogne so we abandoned the idea of that holiday. Sorry though I was for his discomfort I think we were both equally happy to stay at the cottage. Anyway nothing daunted John decided that with the extra time gained by not going away he would install the new stairs.

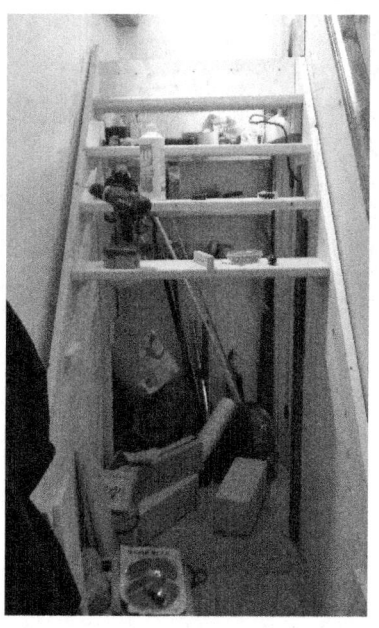

*Work in progress*

*Completed in time for bed!*

This time they came partially in kit form and were installed in one day. John was able to buy the risers and treads, then had a challenging few hours working out spacings and angles. I was anxious that I might not be able to access the upstairs at bedtime, but all was well! A few days later the carpet fitter returned and the stairs were carpeted with the same grey carpet that had been used for the rest of the upstairs.

We had achieved our goal of finishing upstairs in our first year. It had been hard work and with a degree of personal pain for John but also a good deal of satisfaction for both of us.

The cottage is very small with one room downstairs and the downstairs loo and our bedroom upstairs plus the shower room. We would have liked a window on the end wall from which to look out at the fabulous view. There were several possibilities to improve the situation. One was to build an extension on the side of the cottage which would give us more room and could have windows facing the view. That was dismissed on grounds of cost. Secondly we discussed the idea of having a window upstairs in the end wall. There were two things against that. Getting through the very thick wall, almost three feet, would be very difficult and although it was solid stone on both sides in between them is just filled with a jumble of stones which would collapse taking the wall with it if disturbed. So that was not a good idea.

As the autumn progressed another reason for not having a window in the end wall revealed itself and that happened when we had a severe gale and the end wall of the house facing the prevailing gale force winds took a tremendous battering. Not a good place for a window after all.

So with an extension out on grounds of cost and a window out for reasons of common sense we looked into other possible options. This is when the idea of a garden cabin started to look attractive. And when we found one in kit form at an end of season sale at half price it was an offer too good to miss. We bought it at one of the bricolage stores in Mayenne and eagerly awaited its delivery.

When it had been unloaded onto the lawn we were faced with a huge pile of timber. It had to be stored inside over the winter. Half of it went upstairs into our bedroom and half downstairs behind the sofa. The task of lugging it all inside and half of it upstairs was quite arduous and we knew would have to be repeated in reverse the following spring when the time came to put it all together.

There remained one urgent job to do before the end of the summer and that was to start digging again and divert the kitchen drain away from the drive and into the fosse septique. Again Trixie showed great interest in the developing hole but decided that once again her supervisory role was quite sufficient.

*More drainage works*

Now it was autumn and time to turn our attention to the garden and put in new plants. We bought two apple trees and they were planted and watered regularly. Later these were supplemented by two pear trees, an apricot and a Mirabelle plum. Much as we enjoy the fruit the main reason for planting them was to have the gorgeous blossom in the spring.

That first autumn we went up to a nursery near Le Teilleuil which very much impressed us; elsewhere we had been disappointed with the standard of care given to plants waiting to be sold. We planted a Hydrangea paniculata and several perennials in the long border. In the first year or so at the cottage we frequently brought plants from England and gradually the border filled up and it became the real joy that it is today.

That autumn we put tulips in the border for the following spring and also planted daffodils beneath the fruit trees. It is such a pleasure when we come back each March to see the cheerful nodding heads of the daffodils.

My vegetable growing in the border that first summer had been fairly successful so we decided to have a proper French potager and, as is so often the case in France, we had flowers as well as salads, soft fruit and vegetables in it. So an area at the far end of the garden was duly marked out and the grass sprayed. It all looked rather small so before long it was increased in size. Again we knew Trixie would dig there if she had the chance so it had to be fenced and John made a small picket gate for easy access.

Before we went back to England in October of that first year we took delivery of some seasoned logs for the fire.

While the wood was being unloaded from the lorry a small traffic jam of one car developed

on the single track lane in front of the cottage and as I went to apologise in my best French an English voice issued from the car saying,

"What an improvement you've made to the garden."

Thus Gina and Martin came into our lives and we found that like us they had opened their garden in England under the National Garden Scheme. They had moved to live in France permanently a few years earlier and had bought an imposing house near a village about four miles away from us with a lovely walled garden containing fragrant roses and many interesting shrubs. The following summer we enjoyed playing croquet on their lawn and frequently, either at their place or at ours, we met to have a glass of wine.

And then sadly the summer had ended, autumn was well advanced and it was time to go back to England. The long winter months stretched ahead of us but there was to be one more very short visit before the end of the year.

We came back for just two weeks in the middle of December and enjoyed the cosiness of the cottage and evenings spent by our wood burner. During the day I started to dig the potager so that over the winter the frost would break up the soil and when we returned in March we would be able to start planting.

During that time we went to a carol concert organised for English and French people in St Denis de Gastines, a nearby village. It was while we were partaking of the bring and share supper that I started talking to the lady sitting next to me and discovered that amazingly she and her husband lived in Chichester quite close to where we live, as well as having a home in France. Since then we have become firm friends and we often visit each other both in

France and in England.

Then it really was goodbye to the cottage until 2012 but there was plenty to be looking forward to.

\*\*\*\*\*\*\*\*\*\*\*\*\*\*

# Bon Appétit
## Truite au Trou Normande

My friend Judy recommended this recipe which comes from 'The French Kitchen' by Joanne Harris and Fran Warde.

Serves 6

6 trout, gutted and cleaned

100g butter

Sea salt

Freshly ground black pepper

100ml Calvados

Heat the oven to 140°C

Rinse the trout under cold water and dry with kitchen paper.

Melt half of the butter in a large frying pan, add three of the trout and cook on each side for 6 minutes. Place the fish on an oven proof serving plate and keep warm in the oven while you cook the remaining fish. Add them to the serving plate. Pour the Calvados into the frying pan, allow to ignite, pour over the trout and serve at once.

\*\*\*\*\*\*

*A selection of seafood at Super U*

# Chapter Six
## Shopping and Food

I think this is a good point at which to say why a potager is called a potager and to make some observations about going shopping for vegetables in France. First of all and always, it is important to remember how important food is to the French. Good for them I say and shame on people who make a habit of eating nothing but fast food and chips with everything. I love chips. What can be better than egg and chips on a cold day or when you want a quick, filling and tasty meal? And I don't decry 'fast' food totally but let us remember that 'slow' food carefully and lovingly prepared to place before a family can be most rewarding especially if that family is then going to sit down together to eat it and communicate with one another.

Some people are forgetting how to do this in England. We're so busy rushing round, ferrying the children to all their activities that we don't have time to spend in the kitchen. Wouldn't it be better sometimes to slow down and talk to the children?

I love the popularity nowadays of large open plan kitchens where the cook of the day can be busy in the kitchen area while the children are playing on the floor in the living area or doing their homework at a nearby table. Maybe there can be communication about the cooking and the children can do what happened in some families in generations past where the children learned to cook by watching their mothers and joining in. I have recently been reading about the famous chef Raymond Blanc and how much watching his mother cook featured in his life.

It's great today that husbands, dads and partners often share the cooking. My own sons are a case in point. But I don't know how they have taken to cooking because their father's culinary skills are somewhat limited apart from barbecuing. Well now that's a man thing don't you think? But my husband though no cook is great at washing up among many other things as you may have gathered. So we all have our strengths.

So this is what the French are good at, 'slow food', lovingly and carefully prepared. And back to why a potager is called a potager. It's the potage, the soup, which is and was the life and soul of French peasant food. Good, nourishing and filling food and a feast with a hunk of bread and a piece of cheese. And more about cheese anon.

The potagers provide leeks, potatoes, carrots and root vegetables for winter soups and peas, beans, lettuce, courgettes and tomatoes for summer soups. We have raspberries and strawberries too in ours. I know I've missed out lots of things and I'm just remembering the delicious chilled cucumber and yogurt soup I had a craze on making last summer. And the beans of course can be dried and used for winter soups and casseroles as well. The potager needs to have herbs in too for adding to these soups and casseroles.

And still on the subject of soup I watched a

programme on English television recently about harvesting leeks. I was horrified at the wastage that occurred during the harvesting process. A cleverly designed machine yanked the leeks out of the ground, brushed them and gave them an initial trim, so far so good, although more on that later. Within a few minutes the leeks were being processed; more of the green part was cut off and appeared to be going to waste. That's the part I use to make a delicious leek and potato soup.

Another favourite soup is lentil, carrot and tomato. Half fill a large pan with water into which you put several carrots and three handfuls of lentils. Bring to the boil and simmer for twenty minutes. When it has cooled down liquidise with fresh or tinned tomatoes. Add one or two chicken stock cubes or just salt and pepper and herbs from the potager. In Super U they sell largish jars of 'pimento doux moulu' which is paprika so last time I made this soup I added a heaped dessert spoonful of this which enhanced the flavour greatly.

So now a few words about shopping for

vegetables in France. Firstly when you are in the supermarché don't assume you just put the veg in a plastic bag and it will be weighed for you at the till by the cashier or by you if you are at a do-it-yourself till. This could result, and has resulted, in an embarrassing rush back through the shop to weigh your own veg in the greengrocery section while everyone else in your queue, who is now being kept waiting, shrugs their shoulders in a typical Gallic manner whilst muttering under their breath about 'Les Anglaises'. Look at the number on the shelf behind the product you have picked up, take it to the nearby weighing machine, press the right number and 'voila', a ticket will emerge with a bar code on it for you to stick on the plastic bag to be scanned at the till. We all learn from our mistakes.

Secondly the neatly prepared and sanitised veg we are used to buying at supermarkets in England may possibly be found in a French supermarket but far more visible are the 'real' vegetables; this unsurprisingly brings me back to leeks again. You see great stacks of them, straight out of the ground just with the mud knocked off them. By the side is the label 'Poireau plante'. Yes really, a leek plant! So you go back home with them and do a bit of 'slow' work on them. Not just tipping them out of the packet and into the pan. Chop off the root and the coarse leaves at the top and then off you go. Also bunches of unwashed and gritty radishes need slow and frankly tedious attention when you get them home. The lettuce are the same; huge great lettuces ready to go in the larger sized bags provided. They don't need weighing, you buy those as a 'pièce' like cucumbers. Incidentally talking of cucumbers they don't come ready wrapped in cling film as they often do at home. Neither do tomatoes come in packets as we often find them at our supermarkets. They come in great huge piles often with four, five or six tomatoes still on the vine. They come from Brittany, a major vegetable growing area in France, so here they don't have very far to come. Melons and cauliflowers are also piled high. A bit more care is taken with the peaches because they are more delicate but still they are displayed in layers in boxes.

And now for cheese. I remember the days before supermarkets when you went into the grocer's shop and stood in a queue waiting to be served and there on the counter would be a huge block of cheddar cheese on a marble slab with a wire attached to it for slicing through the cheese.

Cheese, mainly cheddar. Maybe there was Stilton at Christmas but I'm not sure we ever had anything as exotic as that. The point I am making is that there was not the variety we have today.

Thirty years ago I was making goat cheese, a rarity, certainly not available in a supermarket anyway at that time, neither was goats' milk which I sold, frozen, thirty pints at a time to my customers who were buying for their children with eczema. How times have changed. Now you can easily buy goats' milk and a large variety of cheeses in the supermarkets in England.

And now to eating and buying cheese in France. I'm not an expert at this. I just make observations. The French eat a lot of cheese. It is said there is one variety for every day of the year. They like to finish their meal with something sweet so the cheese course comes after the main course, le plat principal, and then the dessert follows on. When I have guests for a meal in England or in France I often put the cheese and dessert on the table at the same time then people can choose whether to follow English or French customs. And another slight diversion as we are talking of desserts is the fabulous 'Tarte au Poire' that I often buy at Super U when we are entertaining. It consists of a crisp pastry case lined with frangipane, on top of which are upside down pear halves topped off with a glaze. Delicious!

I think some varieties of cheeses are more popular than others. In the Pays de La Loire, adjacent to Normandy, there are several varieties of Camembert for sale and delicious and creamy it is too. We're not far from Camembert where it is made.

When you open the door of the cheese cabinet quite a strong smell wafts out especially if you have opened the door to the goat cheese section.

Here are just a small number of the cheeses found in the cheese cabinet at our local supermarché. Firstly grated Emmental cheese is sold in packets. Is that a fast food? Next to that is strong Cheddar cheese, yes good old English Cheddar. I don't know if the French buy it, maybe it is there for the English of whom there are quite number in this region. Another hard cheese is Beaufort cheese made in the Alps which is popular with my family and we often take a piece back for them.

Several varieties of goat cheese come next. I usually buy the 'crottins' sold in pairs and very nice for a goat cheese salad with walnuts, figs and honey dribbled over. Sometimes I buy St Maure de Touraine; a name redolent of knights of old. Touraine being the part of the Loire valley centred on Tours, an area containing a high number of French chateaux.

I have enjoyed buying cheese at markets in Provence and the Alps where the crottins come in several forms. You will find mature, very mature and extremely mature, that means they are hard and very mouldy. Extra tasty and smelly if you don't let the appearance put you off.

Now back in the cheese cabinet at Super U the blue cheeses come next. One of our favourites is the Bleu des Causses made high on the plateau south of Millau and east of where Roquefort is made. Bleu des Causses is made from the raw milk of the Montbeliarde and Aubrac breeds of cow and matured in the caves of the Gorges du Tarn. Bleu d'Auvergne and St Agur are also favourites of ours. Roquefort is a seriously strong blue cheese said to be a favourite of the Emperor Charlemagne and to be the cheese of kings and popes. It is made from ewes' milk and like Bleu des Causses is matured in caves in the same region. Another blue cheese is Fourme d'Ambert, one of France's oldest cheeses dating back to Roman times.

One day we met an elderly French man in front of the cheese cabinet having a problem reading his wife's handwriting on the list clutched in his hand. On his list was written 'St Albray'; this is a cheese similar in texture to Camembert but made in a distinctive shape like the six petals of a flower. It very much amused me that we, an English couple, should be helping a Frenchman to buy cheese, but that resulted in us discovering another delicious cheese. And swiftly passing many other marvellous cheeses we come to the end of the cabinet to where Camembert from several different producers is stacked on the shelves.

Naturally in Super U there is also an excellent choice of wines from all over France. The crisp white Loire wines are produced in the Pays de la Loire, the department where our cottage is located but the wine growing area is much further to the south on the slopes of the Loire valley. Although we buy many different wines our favourites are the Rhone wines from areas we have visited such as Gigondas, Vacqueyras, Cairanne and Mont Ventoux.

And one last word about shopping in the supermarché is that pretty well everything you can buy back home can be found here, including the ubiquitous jars of Marmite, tea bags, baked beans and tomato ketchup. You certainly won't starve whether you are just visiting France or have come to live here.

\*\*\*\*\*\*\*\*\*\*\*\*\*

*Cheeses at Super U*

# Bon Appétit
## Pavlova

This is not a specifically French recipe but it's so good with raspberries or strawberries freshly picked from our French garden.

Four egg whites

250g caster sugar

One tablespoon cornflour

2 teaspoons vinegar

A few drops of vanilla essence

284ml double cream

Raspberries or other fruit.

Whisk the egg whites until very stiff, add the sugar a tablespoon at a time. Whisk in the cornflour and the vinegar. Place onto a baking sheet lined with baking parchment, spread into a 23 cm round or whatever suits the plate or pretty glass dish you are serving it from.

Hollow out the centre slightly. Bake in a preheated cool oven at 130°C/ gas mark1. After one and a half hours switch the oven off and leave the Pavlova to cool in the oven, overnight if possible. Whip the cream and pile onto the Pavlova and decorate with your chosen fruit. I like raspberries because their sharp flavour and the cream and meringue go so well together.

\*\*\*\*\*\*\*

# Chapter Seven
## And into our Second Year

So here was a new year, 2012 and this year, not having to wait until June, we needed to plan our allotted time carefully. As UK residents we are allowed to spend six months in France and with house, motor and travel insurance regulations to bear in mind it worked out that no more than sixty days was permitted for each visit. Stay for more than the six months and you may become liable for French taxes and have to register your car in France, and forfeit your access to the National Health Service. Many English people move to live in France permanently but I would say that for anybody doing that it is wise to keep a small pad in England so that you have somewhere to come back to if you change your mind. It can always be let during the time you live in France. This of course, as with everything else, depends on finances but at the moment we're hearing of quite a lot of younger people who have moved out to live the dream and who are finding it difficult to get employment in France.

Also some people buy a property larger than they need because it is so much cheaper in many areas of France than in England. If they do decide to sell it can be difficult. We English tend to go for older properties that we can renovate but there is so much space here that the pressure on land is nowhere near as great as it is in England and it seems that every village has at least one modern bungalow development where each detached property has a  good sized garden around it. This is where the French frequently live, not the older stone properties the English often buy. So if you have bought a large, stone property and then you want to sell a few years later you may have a problem with your sale and if you want to go back to England you may also have a problem getting back on the property ladder at the point at which you hopped off to go to France. Property prices in France are relatively static, not the investment opportunity so often seen in the UK. I should also point out at this juncture that there is talk of putting a twenty percent increase in tax on second homes in areas of housing shortage such as Paris but I don't think that applies elsewhere at the moment.

But for us, six months in France and six months in England is working out very well. We have a life in England and a small property in France which we hope will sell fairly easily when the time arrives. We don't imagine we shall be staying here for a great many years at our age, the longer the better of course, but there has to be some degree of realism when you are in your seventies. Making the most of every day is the best policy.

With all this in mind we created a year planner and filled in our preferred times to be in France, taking note additionally of things we needed to do in England, like medical appointments and family get-togethers. We decided to go out to the cottage in early March. That first trip would last through April, then two or three weeks in the UK, returning to France in mid-May. Then apart from a few days at home in June we would stay until the August trip home for the annual family get-together. We'd go back to the cottage at the end of August, stay until mid-October saving a fortnight for a visit back to France at the end of November; this was mainly to put the garden to bed for the winter. That was roughly the way we hoped the year would work out.

So with great excitement we set off on a chilly March day for France going via the Channel Tunnel because at that time I was still very wary of going by sea but more about that later. As we arrived we were delighted to see that some of the daffodils we had planted the previous autumn were nodding in the breeze and their bright flowers were announcing the arrival of spring. After lighting the wood burner, switching on the electric blankets to air the beds, unpacking and having a meal we started to make a plan of action. It had been wonderful to walk into the cottage and look at the finished work upstairs and to realise just how worthwhile all the hard work of the previous year had been.

First on the list for this second year at the cottage was to do something about the downstairs loo.

Once again there were exposed pipes; worse than that, in the narrow space when you sat on the loo your knees touched the opposite wall. The large basin, installed by the previous owners had been ideal for them when it was the only wash basin before they put in the shower room upstairs but it wasn't necessary for us to have such a large one. Also of course the smallest room needed decorating. A minimalist approach was called for; a compact loo was purchased and a stylish tiny square hand basin which was all that was required. The new loo was relocated and went against the end wall so the knees-touching-the-wall situation was a thing of the past. John had discovered that plenty of space had been left between the plasterboard and the outside wall; he would use that space by fixing the basin in it and adding

a large mirror over the basin. With clever lighting he created an artificial window in the windowless room. We even rigged up a faux roller blind with a silk tassel to enhance the effect. The 'roller blind' was made from paper that matched the rather flamboyant wall paper we had chosen for two walls. Normally we choose magnolia paint or in the case of the cottage fresh white paint but in the downstairs loo we decide to go a bit wild and have intertwining pink flowers on a cream background for the wallpaper and paint the other wall pink to match the flowers. Cheerful! The occasional blue tile set among the existing white tiles did not look good with the new scheme so John carefully cut out squares from the wall paper and stuck them on the blue tiles. Grey lino on the floor completed the effect and we were very pleased with the result.

The cabin had been stored overwinter in the cottage and we were keen to get it out of the way, partly because it was occupying a lot of space but also because some English friends were coming to stay at the beginning of April. They were prepared to camp on the lawn but as the cabin was almost underway and would be more comfortable for them we decided to push on and get it finished.

Before we had returned to the UK in December we had pegged out an area for the concrete base as far back in the car parking area as we could go and we had arranged that Stuart would come in the middle of March to help John lay the concrete for the base. The day before he arrived we realised we had chosen the wrong position for the cabin because if we kept to our original plans there was no place to park the car where it would not be blocking the view to some extent. It would be just the same as it had been during our caravan holidays when the car was parked next to the caravan on a camp site. So almost at the last minute we moved the position forward to within the fence Stuart had erected at the end of the garden. Afterwards we were so glad we had done that because it increased the parking space and gave a useful working area behind the cabin for collecting garden debris and having the occasional bonfire. The new position was perfect at the end of the lawn and now the car could be parked behind out of the way.

Stuart duly came and the concrete base was satisfactorily laid. When it had hardened off the work on erecting the cabin started, first carrying it out of the cottage and along the garden piece by piece, laying the sturdy planks out in the right sequence for ease of construction and then slotting them all together. It was quite a job but it all fitted together well and the cabin took shape fairly quickly. By the time our friends arrived the cabin was weatherproofed and two folding beds had been installed for them. We'd put some carpet remnants and a rug on the floor and it was deemed to be better than sleeping in a tent on wet grass. Having achieved quite a lot in the month we had been at the cottage we were able to enjoy some time off with our friends.

We decided to go and explore Fougères. The previous year we had discovered a fascinating enterprise called 'Emmaus' on the outskirts of Fougères. There is a network of these shops, in France and internationally, where you can buy second hand articles of all kinds. The Emmaus movement was started in France in 1949 by a priest, Abbé Pierre, to help combat poverty and homelessness. It helps people who are in poverty and socially excluded to use and develop skills to make changes for the better in their lives and the communities in which they live. Renovated furniture and all kinds of second hand goods are sold in their shops. This provides for the needy in terms of employment, housing and financial aid, and is a useful way to recycle one's redundant possessions.

So our visit to Emmaus at Fougères turned out to be an entry into a treasure trove of furniture, china, cutlery, old linen sheets, second hand clothes, records, books and all sorts of other things. Quite an amazing place where you could pick up incredible bargains. John, who has a penchant for snails, had been looking for some  traditional dishes for serving them in, heavy ceramic two handled dishes with twelve holes in which to cook and serve the snails. I think he had located some on the internet, but they were very expensive. We were pleased when we found some at Emmaus for just two euros for eight dishes. 'For all of them?' I queried. 'Oui, madame,' the sales person answered. We couldn't believe the low price. I also bought some rustic pottery dishes.

I examined some old linen sheets much sought after by some collectors and was very tempted to buy but not this time I decided

Over a period of time we took several unwanted items from the cottage to Emmaus; the small fridge and a microwave amongst them.

We were very amused to discover that there was an unofficial recycling depot very much closer to home, at the end of the lane in fact by the poubelles. (Did you know that French dustbins are named after a certain Monsieur Poubelle, 1831-1907, lawyer, administrator and diplomat and préfet of the Seine region?) For example, the cane garden furniture which we used inside the cottage; within an hour of taking the first chair up to the poubelles site it had gone, no doubt to appear in someone's vide grenier or brocante sale. It was just the same when the remainder of the cane furniture went up there. And when John took some heavy velvet curtains there, helpfully putting on the measurements for interested persons, they too disappeared very quickly. Many items have been 'freecycled' in this way; when John has nothing better to do he plans to hide in the nearby bushes to observe proceedings!

While our friends were still with us for their first visit we decided to show them the delights of the local small town, Gorron. It's a fairly unremarkable little place but has an impressive church dominating the town at the top of the hill. The spire can be seen from the cottage as can the spire of the village church not far away in Brecé, both of them floodlit at night.

But the interesting thing about Gorron for us is that it is twinned with Hayling Island which is only just along the road from us in Chichester in the Portsmouth direction. A sign in front of the Gorron Mairie tells you it is only one hundred and eighty seven miles or three hundred kilometres away, quite close really. The sign also tells you that Gorron is twinned with Schwaikheim in Germany and that, at nine hundred and seventy four kilometres distance, is considerably further away. You can't help applauding the sense of forgiveness and reconciliation behind this particular twinning. Apparently after the Second World War some German prisoners from Schwaikheim were held in Gorron and were treated with such kindness that they wanted to come back to visit afterwards and out of that arose the twinning idea. Amid many of the horrors perpetrated in our life time there is still kindness and a sense of humanity to be found.

In the first week of April spring was beginning to get going. One of my favourite poems from my junior school teaching days was 'The Jabberwocky' by Lewis Carroll. I love the lines

'Oh frabjous day.
Callooh! Callay!

In the poem 'the beamish boy' had killed the Jabberwocky but I love the nonsense words in the poem and when the sun shines and everything is wonderful with the world I feel like saying 'Oh frabjous day, Callooh! Callay!'

*Tulips in Fougères*

As April progressed there were a lot of frabjous days. The tulips in the public park that overlooks the massive chateau at Fougères being a case in point; wonderful colourful displays promoting a sense of well-being.

There were celandines glowing in the valley by the river, the sunlight sparkling on the cascading water near the old mill. Later, bluebells and white stitchwort flowered, dainty against the fresh green grass. Golden pis-en–lit, literally 'wet the bed' (dandelions) already attracting bees and butterflies. There were swathes of ladies smock which is the principal larval foodstuff for the orange tip butterflies which were also observed in abundance on the water meadows by the river.

Many white butterflies were also among them and I discovered they were the female orange tips, the males of the species flaunting themselves as if so often the case in the natural world.

But I think what gave me the most joy was the sight of the wild cherry trees with their clouds of white blossom in the hedgerows. This may have dated from my childhood when in May I enjoyed walking to school under avenues of cherry trees with their blossom defined against the blue sky above.

From our vantage spot in the garden we view many miles of countryside extending into the distance; pristine white cherry blossom can be seen scattered like wedding veils along the

hedgerows and punctuating the fresh green canopies of oaks, chestnut and poplars. White blossom is there too in Camille Pissarro's painting of 'La Maison Rose' and Monet's 'Springtime'.

That spring we discovered the 'Pissarro Trail' at a village near Ambrières called Montfaucault. It's a small hamlet where he stayed with a friend and painted. Along the walk, which circles the village on a path through woodland and alongside fields, easels have been set up displaying prints of the scene as he painted it from that particular spot. Enchanting to a lover of Impressionist paintings such as myself.

At the end of April the time was fast approaching when we would once more be on our way back home to England. Before we left there was the dismantling of what we had dubbed 'The Ginger Boxes'. These were strange and complex constructions put on the ceiling to disguise firstly where the hole had been for the ladder into what was then the hay loft, later to become the bedroom, and secondly to disguise where the chimney had been from the original fireplace. A few months later when the wood burner and flue were being dismantled and the area cleared for the new wood burner we could see on the wall the outline of the huge fireplace that had once been there. In the early days of the cottage this would have been where all the cooking was done; it's most likely it was an open fire but later might have been a cast iron range with the central fire and an oven each side with hot plates on the top for cooking. I've seen that in a four hundred and fifty year old cottage in England. It would not have been the original there and maybe our cottage always had an open fire for cooking and providing heat; we were told that at some period these old fireplaces went out of fashion. I suppose they were impractical with a lot of the heat escaping up the chimney. Anyway that and the mantelpiece above it had all gone and before electricity came to this area a sort of pre-Aga type of white enamel range cooker had been installed with a stove pipe flue. It must have been very modern in its day. This had been removed and replaced with a gas cooker using bottled gas. A wood burner with a brick surround had also been installed.

The ceiling above this had been covered with a pine box arrangement, the colour of the wood being quite out of keeping with the dark old beams. So that was dismantled exposing the hidden stout beams. John was able to match the paint used on the main beams, giving a much less intrusive finish. A simple piece of white plaster board also replaced the ginger pine box on the other side of the room. Dismantling that held some horrors, for when it was taken down we found it had been lined with insulation material which over the years had provided a home for rats and was full of their droppings. I had been sleeping in ignorance above this from the time we had been here. It was good to have it gone. The whole room looked better for these modifications. And then it was time to go back to England for much of May.

\*\*\*\*\*\*\*\*\*\*\*\*\*

# Bon Appétit
## Moules Marinière

As we are near the border of Brittany and Normandy I have to include this typical Breton dish. Cultivated mussels grow on the sea bed on stakes called bouchots in the Bay of Mont St Michel.

Buy the quantity you need, making sure they are closed, and clean them thoroughly. Put them in a big bowl of cold water and leave for a few minutes. Discard any that float as they are dead.

Melt 50g of butter, soften two or three shallots without browning them. Add white wine, a bay leaf, pepper and a little salt. Simmer gently for ten minutes. Add the mussels and stir until they are all open, discard any that do not open. Serve with freshly chopped parsley, bread for mopping up the juices and traditionally a glass of Muscadet.

# Chapter Eight
## Summer in France

When we came back towards the end of May it was with renewed vigour so that we could reach our target of getting the cottage renovated by the end of this, our second year. But life was not all work by any means and every afternoon we took the dog for a walk.

It had been a great joy to us to find the river at the end of the lane, something we hadn't known about when we bought the cottage;

then to discover a network of paths running alongside it was a great bonus. One of the circuits came up from the village, along the lane and then down to the old mill at Pont à Bouty, across the bridge and back to the village through the meadows.

This old mill, one of three in this section, had been Brecé mill and between the mill and Brecé were the remnants of an ancient footpath just above the flood plain. It is a narrow path winding through the woods, just wide enough for a man and a pack animal to carry the sacks of grain or flour. Records show that the mill at Pont à Bouty was there before the French Revolution and a picture on the nearby information board shows that it was in use as late as 1906 and that people were living in adjacent cottages perched on the rocks out of reach of the flood water.

*Photos on the next page*

*An old photo of the Brecé mill*
*And as it is today*

The census figures for 1906 give the miller's
name as Auguste Chabrun who was born at

Gorron in 1879, but he was the last miller as by the time of the 1911 census the mill was no longer in use.

In 1841 the miller was Charles Foucher, a widower. Five years later Napoleon Renault aged thirty-three was the miller and he was still there at the 1861 census. In 1866 Benjamin Chabrun aged thirty-eight was the miller and he was still there ten years later. By 1881 there had been a change and Theophile Arnouls aged thirty-six was the miller but he only appeared on that census. By 1886 Pascal Lelandais had taken over and he was still there in 1901 and then Auguste Chabrun took over until the mill closed down. It's quite likely that he was a descendant of the Benjamin Chabrun who had been the miller in earlier years.

Now the mill is a ruin and the mill wheel gone but in time of heavy rain the water still rushes through the mill race and you can almost imagine the huge wooden wheel turning away and grinding the flour. The river Colmont has a very extensive catchment area, essentially a plateau reaching a height of six hundred feet or so. The river flows quite vigorously even throughout the drier summer months and with considerable force during the winter. The level rises very quickly after heavy rains, and the location of several mills in this section of the river reflects its power and reliability as a source of energy in the past.

The footpath that goes over the Pont à Bouty also turns to the left and makes its way down the valley, mostly alongside the river, passing Le Moulin de Favières, a medieval mill which worked by electricity in its later years and closed in 1984. This mill was owned by the Seigneur de Favières who lived in a moated manor house a mile away from the river. There is a small chapel next to the manor house and there are several stone buildings nearby. The whole settlement has come down in the world, bicycles are kept in the chapel and some of the moat has disappeared. Further along the river is the Moulin Neuf constructed in 1870, a working mill until 1964.

Soon after that by the Saut au Loup the track turns uphill and joins a higher lane. A notice board at that point by the river tells you that this is where in about 1863 the last wolf in the department of Mayenne jumped across the river to escape from the hounds owned by the Seigneur de Favière. A large stone in the middle of the river is where the wolf leapt to safety and thence to the other side thus escaping. The story goes that from then on it never returned to the lands of the Seigneur de Favière preferring to stay on the other side where the land belonged to the Seigneur du Châtaignier. A wise wolf obviously.

This is one of our favourite walks; leaving the Saut au Loup behind us we turn up a steep hill and onto the lane which takes us back towards Brecé and past the Manoir de Châtaignier, an imposing manor house with two round towers with turrets, dating from the time of the Hundred Years War between the English and the French. This part of the walk is along a very quiet lane with a wide variety of wild flowers on its verges throughout the spring and summer months; there are wonderful views over the surrounding fields and woodland. After nearly a mile the path goes down a steep track to the river and then either to Brecé or back to Pont à Bouty.

It was one afternoon after such a walk that on the spur of the moment we decided to put into action a possibility we had talked about for some time which was exchanging the bulky wood burner for something smaller and more elegant. The existing wood burner was on a brick platform with a storage space for logs underneath and had a brick wall on three sides. There was a safety element in this in that when coming through the adjacent door you wouldn't be able to come into contact with the hot casing of the wood burner. However we felt that would not be a problem with a smaller 'poêle à bois'. So there we were, just returned from the walk and with the kettle on the boil for the afternoon cup of tea, when we decided to 'go for it'. John fetched his sledge hammer and 'Bang!' there was the first section of the wall down. By the end of the afternoon the brick work had been demolished and the wood burner was dismantled and outside.

This was a fortuitous decision; the old wood burner had been temperamental and very smoky at times. The reason was only too obvious, the flue pipe leading to the chimney was seriously blocked. Cleaning and re-routing the pipe to avoid right angle bends ensured a much better performance. Once we have an idea we go for it!

That is if we are in agreement about what we are going for, otherwise John goes silent and waits for me to get over whatever mad idea has entered my head. However on this occasion we were united in thought and by the next day John began to prepare the area for the new wood burner. We could now see part of the outline of the original fire place and realised how huge it must have been in that small room. In the photo below, taken at the Brecé

Ecomusée, you can see what a typical cottage room of that era must have looked like with the large fireplace on the far side.

By the end of the month a new, neat and efficient but far more attractive wood burner had been installed and we could envisage cold autumn evenings when we would be very cosy. In fact in time it turned out to be a bit too cosy and John made a vent in the ceiling to let surplus hot air go into the bedroom above.

So with that part of the room now painted white we pressed on to change the rest of the kitchen area from lemon yellow to white and then moved on to cover the coffee coloured walls in the rest of the room with fresh white paint. What a huge difference that made. The room now looked larger and lighter and the white walls contrasted well with the dark beams.

There was ginger coloured pine panelling on the lower half of the walls round the side of the room where we had our sofa and arm chair. The pine panelling needed finishing off with beading and then all of it was painted white. It took several coats of paint but again the white wood work was very fresh and attractive.

The previous Christmas we had given ourselves three framed prints of Pissarro's paintings of rural French scenes. These were hung on the walls and we were nearly there.

It was around this time that we made our second trip to Ikea at Rennes and bought a dark bureau which had useful cupboard space; we also bought a drop leaf table. When we came to the cottage we kept the dining table used by the previous owners but it occupied quite a lot of space, something which was in short supply in our one up, one down home.

So the drop leaf table, cleverly fitted with three drawers on either side, gave the room a much more spacious feel and provided some much needed storage.

Now that the amount of work remaining to be done on the cottage was much reduced we allowed ourselves to be tourists from time to time. One August day we set off for Sainte Suzanne, south of Mayenne. We had Trixie with us and on the way there found a lovely woodland glade in which to stop for a picnic. We got out of the car and were immediately assailed by three of the sweetest tiny kittens rushing towards us and meowing pitifully.

'Take us home, rescue us', they wailed as they scampered across the woodland floor towards us. Poor little mites, they had obviously been dumped there, no doubt very recently. Sadly there was nothing we could do to help them. We had no cat carrying facilities with us, didn't know where to take them if we had and furthermore had a gentle greyhound with us that turned into a ferocious monster if she ever caught sight of a cat. We felt awful driving away and often wondered what became of them.

This is a not infrequent occurrence in France. In rural areas people don't get their cats spayed and many unwanted kittens are born and subsequently abandoned. The English are a soft touch where these cats are concerned and we know several English people who have taken them in and have numerous cats as a result. One friend feeds the cats from the farm next door so she can slip contraceptives into their food and thus control the cat population in that locality.

After that episode we continued with our trip to Sainte Suzanne. It is described as 'La Petite Cité de Caractère et l'un des plus Beaux Villages de France'. Yes it is a very attractive place with a lovely chateau. Unfortunately we could not visit the chateau as we had Trixie with us and it was too hot to leave her in the car. On a different occasion we visited a chateau in the Loire that we were able to take her into but more of that anon.

However on that hot day in August she was able to join on the next part of the tourist trail which was to the nearby Camp of William the Conqueror, 'le Camp de Guillaume le Conquèrant', which unlike the tourist hotspot of Sainte Suzanne was totally deserted so we had it to ourselves. It consisted of two large rectangular areas, each about the size of a football pitch, enclosed by high earth ramparts from which there was a good view of Sainte Suzanne 800 metres away. We read that in attempting to extend his kingdom into Maine William had conquered the chateaux of Le Mans and elsewhere. Then having set his sights on Sainte Suzanne his army besieged the place unsuccessfully between 1083 and 1086 and finally went home with their tails between their legs. William was only there for part of the time and died in 1087, his great survey of England, the Domesday Book, having been completed the preceding year.

I had previously thought he was fully occupied in England after 1066 but apparently not all the time; in fact he spent much of the last fifteen years of his life in Normandy. So by the time of the siege of Sainte Suzanne he was King of England and it wasn't his kingdom of Normandy he was trying to enlarge it was his kingdom of England in France.

His great grandson Henry Plantagenet, 1133-1189, was already count of Anjou by inheritance from his father when he acceded to the throne of England in 1154 and he was Duke of Aquitaine by right of his wife Eleanor and he also ruled almost half of medieval France. This encompassed land from the Pyrenees up through Gascony, Anjou and Normandy. His son John was born in 1167 and he was King of England from 1199 until his death in 1216, the year after the English Barons made him sign Magna Carta. He was defeated by Philip the Second of France thus losing Normandy and Anjou. The English retained Gascony but the scene was set for the Hundred Years War.

We also visited St Céneri-le-Gérei a village in the Alpes-Mancelles right in the south of the Orne department of Lower Normandy.

The River Sarthe flows through the area which is very beautiful. I believe it is the only village in France to have an Englishman as its mayor.

Soon after that in August it was time to go back to England and our annual weekend with the family. It is always good to see everybody together again and now increasingly as the grandchildren grow up we are aware that some years someone will be off travelling or working and the times when we are all together may be limited. This particular week end we had a meal at the hotel at Goodwood which was delightful and the next day were all together again at our home in Chichester.

Then before long we went back to France and at the end of August the final touches were given to the kitchen. The white tiles were replaced with honey coloured ones and John put a narrow shelf above them on which we displayed our blue and white plates and hung pretty mugs underneath.

On the wall we displayed some copper saucepans and a very old willow pattern plate that had been in my family for years. An LED light strip under the shelf was the final touch and we were delighted. We had achieved our goal of renovating the cottage in two years.

We continued to enjoy our walks with Trixie and from time to time met another new friend both for her and for us. Trixie's new friend was Frisbee, an eight year old Border Collie/Lurcher cross who is a handsome friendly dog. We often meet him and his owner Judy when we are walking in the valley and also when they walk along our lane and pass the cottage when Trixie rushes excitedly to the fence in a frenzy of barking. It wasn't long before the dogs were getting on so well together that Frisbee and Judy came into the garden and the dogs enjoyed romps together. Judy and her husband have a house in the valley and live in France for part of the year as we do. Thus the circle of friends we have made in France grows.

*Frisbee: Photo courtesy of Jerry Fraser*

Meanwhile work had been progressing in the garden. More lavender hedging had been planted, the border was colourful and was filling up with shrubs and perennials, sometimes the plants having travelled out with us from England. The potager was very productive and we had salads, vegetables, strawberries and raspberries.

Where the ugly stone bench had been John had made a small bower to hold two garden chairs side by side and the following year we planted a rose either side of it, the wonderfully scented 'Madame Alfred Carrière' and they are growing well. The pretty, creamy flowers have pale pink

*Productive potager*

buds that gradually change colour as the flowers open. An absolute joy.

We decided to have a pergola next to the bower; this provides support to several vines giving the effect of going through a leafy tunnel when leaving the cottage and walking into the main part of the garden.

My next project was to have a bed planted mainly with grasses, the idea being to have plants that would not require watering. So in the autumn a patch of lawn was sprayed out next to the pergola and the new bed was ready for planting the following spring.

All this hard work deserved a little holiday so we took ourselves off to the Loire Valley for a short break. We found a hotel at Chinon to which we were able to take Trixie. The bedroom was excellent but the spiral staircase up to it was not dog friendly and poor John ended up carrying twenty-nine kilograms of dog up the last section. Not good.

The hotel was right by the River Vienne six miles upstream from where it joins the Loire and it was pleasant to walk alongside the river with Trixie.

We visited the chateau at Langeais and were pleased and surprised to find that Trixie was allowed to go in as well. Our blue-grey greyhound looked very elegant going up the wide stone stairs and we were very amused when in one of the grand rooms another visitor pointed out her resemblance to the hunting dogs in the tapestries that were hanging on the walls. Exactly so!

*Early morning by the river in Chinon*

*Trixie and (below) her forbears seen on the tapestry*

*The chateau at Langeais*

The highlight of the trip was the visit to the chateau and gardens at Villandry the following morning. This was our second visit having been there some years earlier. The chateau is magnificent and the terraces provide a bird's eye view of the spectacular gardens with their geometrically laid out beds full of colour, using a combination of flowers and vegetables.

We ended our visit with a simple lunch at a nearby restaurant and then turned for home just over two hours away. Lovely though our visits to both chateaux and the beautiful gardens at Villandry had been we were glad to be back in our humble peasant's cottage, enjoying our peaceful garden.

In September our friends came to see us again, once more 'camping' in the cabin at the end of the garden. In addition to the electricity and Wi-Fi that had been installed there for the first visit they now had dark blue roller blinds because last time there had been a full moon shining out of a clear sky for each night of their visit and it was a bit like trying to sleep under a spotlight.

We had a splendid meal at our favourite restaurant near Mayenne and then went down river to one of the locks. The level of the river is allowed to fall every two years to allow it to be cleared of debris and old cars; it was strange to see so much of the river bed exposed.

This is the River Mayenne, lending its name to the department of the same name. It joins with the River Sarthe and its tributary the Loir, not to be confused with the Loire, to form the River Maine which is seven miles long, flows through the city of Angers and then joins the River Loire. This, the longest river in France, rises in the Massif Central in the Cevennes, first flowing northwards for six hundred and twenty miles through Nevers to Orléans then west through Tours and Nantes and finally into the Bay of Biscay. It also gives its name to the area in which our cottage is, the Pays de la Loire.

The Loire throughout history has been a major trading route and here we were with our friends on the towpath that goes between Mayenne and Laval. In the sixteenth century works were undertaken to make the Mayenne navigable between Chateau-Gontier and Laval, meaning the wines from the Loire region could be transported to Laval. Between 1853 and 1868 further works were undertaken, by means of constructing locks, such as the one we were visiting, to make the river navigable as far as the town of Mayenne. In the nineteenth century boats up to a hundred and forty tons could navigate the river. They brought construction materials such as wood and stone, coal from the mines at L'Huisserie, grains, fruit and vegetables. Surely wine as well I hear you ask? Oh yes, I should think so.

From the old chateau high above the river in Mayenne there is a panoramic view of the river below and the quays which at one time were bustling with traders unloading boats. On the same side of the river is the Basilique Notre-Dame des Miracles, severely damaged during the Second World War as was much of the town of Mayenne.

We visited the village of Fontaine Daniel, the birthplace of Mayenne textiles, which is four kilometres west of Mayenne. In 1205 an abbey was founded in a clearing in the forest by Cistercian monks from Clairmont Abbey just outside Laval. In 1791 just after the French Revolution the abbey was sold off as a national asset. When we went there cows were being kept in the remains of the abbey church. Times change!

Much of the site was bought by a group of entrepreneurs who set up a spinning mill there. As time went on accommodation was built for the workers and overseers; the cottages had their own gardens and the streets were named after the flowers and animals that are to be found in the local countryside. The Chapel of St Michel, set above the lake, was built in 1939 from granite quarried on the site and today has some wonderful modern stained-glass windows. There is a pleasant green area in the centre of the village and two eateries are nearby.

Mayenne Textiles, Toiles de Mayenne, has been situated at Fontaine Daniel for two hundred years. Near the village is a fascinating showroom where the textiles are displayed and can also be purchased. At the back of the showroom is a large room where remnants can be sifted through and bought. This is a good place to find a bargain. On several occasions I have bought some of the soft, colourful fabrics which I have used to make cushion covers for the cottage and as Christmas presents

# Bon Appétit
## Goat Cheese and Fig Salad

Lettuce, the quantity depends on how much you like lettuce, plus any other salad ingredients of your choice.

St Maure de Touraine or Crottins

One ripe fig per person

Walnut halves

Runny honey

Carefully wash the lettuce and place on the plate with the other salad ingredients tossed in a little olive oil. Slice some of the St Maure de Touraine cheese or halve the crottins horizontally and then cut each half across again. Add to the salad with the quartered figs and the walnuts. Drizzle the honey over the top of the salad. A variation on this is to put the halved crottins on a small slice of baguette drizzled with olive oil and placed in the oven for a few minutes until the cheese is just starting to melt.

I suggest that a crisp white chilled Loire wine is ideal with this meal which should ideally be eaten in the garden under a sunshade on a warm summer day. A meal like this is always best shared with friends.

# Chapter Nine
## The End of Year Two

After a few weeks at home in England we went back to France at the end of November for our final visit of the year. One of our first events was to have Gina and Martin over to a meal. We had enjoyed many happy times together either here at the cottage or at their home and in the summer had been introduced to the delights of playing croquet on their lawn. Now we were to meet for one last time this year and so with our new wood burner alight we enjoyed another few hours of their company.

During the next few days the weather was still good and one day we set off for the six mile walk that we had long promised ourselves we would do. This involved crossing the river lower down and making another, but longer, round walk. We started off by the old Brecé mill at Pont à Bouty and turned left along the path that ran alongside the river through the meadows. Near to the Favière Mill we passed the spot where Trixie enjoyed a dip in the river on hot days. We were amazed the first time she did it. She was paddling in the river near the bank and then just lay down in the water to cool off. I think although the air temperature was hot the water was quite chilly but it seemed to be just what she wanted. Trixie generally does just what Trixie wants to do.

However river bathing was not on the agenda on that November day so on we went passing Moulin Neuf on the other side of the river and on our side a small deserted cottage once lived in by a previous miller. We continued past the Saut au Loup and up the steep hill where the track makes a hairpin bend and far below through the pine trees there is a view of the river tumbling through the gorge on its way to quieter stretches. At one time there had been a bridge by the Saut au Loup but that was long gone, its rusty iron girders just visible in the undergrowth.

We continued onto the lane where usually we turned back towards the Manoir de Châtaignier but today we turned the other way. Our route took us along quiet lanes, past a couple of minor settlements and after a mile or so we turned down a track that led down to the river again. The valley was a little wider at this point and there were fields where cattle often grazed. The land rose steeply and we admired the beautiful autumn colours of the old trees on the slopes. We crossed the plank bridge and passed the ruin of yet another mill. There was plenty of water power in this valley and it has long been exploited by the people who have lived in the valley throughout history.

After crossing the bridge the path curved round the hillside, skirted a farm with noisy dogs and a selection of animals, including a pot-bellied pig. It then joined a quiet lane close to the Dolmen du Petit Vieux Sou, a megalithic tomb dating from 2,400 B.C. It just makes you realise how far back settlement goes in this valley, at least five thousand years, probably longer.

Had we gone the other way along by the river we would have crossed another riverside meadow and then climbed up through the woods and come to the grounds of Chateau d'Isle. We had done this walk several times and the walk up through the beautiful old woodland was very enjoyable with glimpses of the river far below.

*Old Woodland*

*Chateau d'Isle*

However there was a near disaster one day when there were a number of cows in the meadow at the top of the wood. Normally Trixie takes no notice of the cows and the cows take no notice of her but on this occasion there was a cow lying across the path and Trixie barked at it. That made the other cows come over to investigate so we beat a hasty retreat to the small cattle grid which lay between that field and the track that led up to the chateau. Unfortunately it wasn't only the cows that had come to investigate what the dog was barking at because in trying to leave the cattle grid we found an unkempt horse was blocking our way. I attempted to push the horse out of the way and the horse attempted to bite and kick the dog. John set off at a fair pace up the track with the horse after him, head down attempting to bite the dog's tail. Amid a cloud of dust I watched my poor husband, aged seventy, running into the distance.

There was no way I could do anything to help at this stage. About fifty yards away he could see a piece of string across the track and this was all that was stopping the horse escaping. John made for this and in trying to roll underneath it fell and broke the string. I was going along as fast as I could and saw him lying on the ground, still valiantly holding onto the dog. We both thought that the horse would now bite and, or kick the two of them and were most surprised and relieved when the animal saw a succulent patch of grass and sauntered off happily to eat it, the chase and the intended victims forgotten, thank goodness.

Poor John picked himself up, dusted himself down and when he had recovered his breath we continued on our way. It was a very unfortunate incident and could have had disastrous results. Bites and kicks from a horse don't bear thinking about. It rather put us off that particular walk.

But to come back to our long walk on that November day we were now back on our own side of the valley and were about to enter the 'Zone Humide', a pretty section of the walk which goes by the side of the cascading river and climbs upward through the woodland eventually emerging onto the farmland at the top.

*Zone Humide*

It's such a joy to walk in the dappled shade under the trees on a sunny day and listen to the bird song and the river gurgling on its way. We're not far from the Saut au Loup at this point and here the valley is quite narrow and the gradient of the river a little steeper.

*Zone Humide*

As with other sections of the valley there are information boards every so often. Here it gives information about the flora and fauna which can be seen, among which are damsel flies, frogs, spiders and salamanders. We once caught sight of a handsome black and yellow salamander as we walked along this path. I had never seen one before.

We frequently do sections of this long walk as mini round walks either starting out from the cottage or driving a short distance, parking and doing a round back to the car.

But today going through the Zone Humide we were continuing on foot all the way. Soon after emerging from the woodland onto a track which gradually climbed through fields we passed a huge farm building named by one of our neighbours as La Grande Porcherie. This is where pigs are reared intensively and hearing the piggy squeals and detecting a rather distinct aroma that assails your nostrils you can't miss it as you pass by. It's not one of our favourite parts of the walk but soon after that it's out onto a path across the open fields and after a mile gradually down again to the river at Pont à Bouty and then up the lane to our cottage.

Just as we join the lane we come across the ruined place called La Closerie, lived in by successive families; there is evidence of it once having had electricity but it is now a total ruin. Even since we have been at our cottage the roof of La Closerie has further collapsed and now the walls are disintegrating too. As mentioned earlier these older properties are not much sought after by the local population so are allowed to fall into a ruinous state.

The French inheritance laws can be the cause of some places being neglected for years. When the owner dies the property has to be shared among the descendants and sometimes tracing them all can prove to be impossible. Therefore the years pass and the property falls into disrepair and finally becomes an unwanted ruin with no known owner.

We were glad the weather had been suitable for us to do this walk as it had been on our agenda for some time. I was also glad to have done this long walk as I was about to enter a period when, regrettably, walking would not be so easy for me.

The next day while the weather held, John was able to start dealing with the overgrown trees at the end of the garden. You may remember that two years ago when we first saw the cottage we couldn't tell where our far boundary was because it was so overgrown. During our first spring while John was so busy inside I got out my secateurs and a saw and started to hack away at the jungle. Not only did I discover the ancient privy in the corner next to our neighbour's land but realised that by the time this clearance had finished we would have gained about an extra eight feet or so of land. Well there was only so much I could do but at least I had made a start and now two years later John came along to do the heavy work.

Many years earlier someone had planted box bushes at the end of the garden to make a hedge and there were two or three bay trees as well. What with the inevitable ivy twining itself round everything and years of neglect a real jungle had developed. So with the initial clearance done it was now time to deal with the trees that had started out as a box hedge. John has a very useful tool which is an extending lopper with a small saw attached to the end of it. As the branches fell I began to heave them out of the way. That was a mistake as I began to find out the next day when we went for our customary afternoon walk. After fifteen minutes or so I felt a tightening at the bottom of my back on one side. If I stretched my left knee upwards it eased it as did sitting down for a few minutes. If only I had gone for some physiotherapy as soon as we got home that November I might have been saved months of pain later but no, I was sure it would get better on its own.

Anyway the trees were reduced to a manageable height and there was a huge bonfire; where there had been a jungle earlier there was now a straggly line of stick-like vegetation which over the coming months and years would thicken up and become a neat hedge again.

We were now into the last few days of

November and the days and nights had turned frosty. We covered up the dahlias at the front of the potager with brushwood from the tree cutting and pegged it all down under a plastic tunnel. The garden was a sad shadow of its summer glory but we planted more tulips in the long border and thought of the pleasure they would give us in the spring and the new grass bed that I would be planting.

The dog wore her bright red winter coat, we wore woolly hats and gloves and we walked through the frosty fields where a few trees hung onto their last few russet leaves which glowed in the afternoon sun. The river flowed lugubriously on its way, drifts of fallen brown leaves swirled past with the current and the occasional coypu left a V shaped trail behind it returning to its river side burrow. The cows had been taken to their winter quarters and the meadows were quiet and empty. The world was hunkering down ready for the snows of winter.

*Autumn*

*The end of our second year at the cottage*

\*\*\*\*\*\*\*\*\*\*\*\*\*\*

# Bon Appétit
## Tarte aux Poires

Line a flan dish with short crust pastry. There is no need to bake it blind.

Use very ripe pears or gently poach some pears in a little water with a vanilla pod and a little sugar. Peel, core and quarter the pears. Dry them and arrange on the pastry in a circle radiating out from the centre.

To make the frangipane mix 50g sugar with 50g butter, 50g ground almonds, 1 teaspoon flour and one egg. Place this on and around the pears.

Cook in the oven at 180°C/gas 4 until the pastry is crisp and the frangipane is a golden brown.

Eat while warm with crème fraiche or vanilla ice cream.

# Chapter Ten
## And so begins Year Three and beyond with the Chimney, the Fosse, the Garden and a spot of Tourism

So keen was I to get my new grass bed planted that when we went back to France in the last week of March 2013 I donned an old plastic mac and got stuck into the job as soon as I could. It was a pouring wet day and getting stuck into it can be taken literally as I and the mac soon became well covered in mud, so much so that John hosed me down at the end of the planting session.

Although this was ostensibly a grass bed it was in fact a collection of plants which would survive in dry conditions, not need watering and be very low maintenance, So I planted Stipa gigantea, Stipa tenuissima, sedums, euphorbias, Verbena bonariensis and thyme to name but a few. As is the way with a newly planted bed it all looked a bit sparse at first so

I bought a few pots of Tête-a-tête daffodils already in flower to cheer it all up. The bed matured amazingly quickly and even by later that summer the grasses had grown beautifully and were swaying in the breeze of which we get a fair amount being near the top of a hill. The Verbena bonariensis and sedums were attracting loads of bees and butterflies which is partly why we had chosen them.

Inside the cottage a few days later a new problem presented itself when a nasty, tarry liquid started to drip from the concrete block on the wall near the wood burner just by the new plate shelf. The concrete block was the remains of the flue of the original fireplace and this liquid was coming down the chimney. Now that we were having more fires a layer of tar and condensation had built up and on careful examination you could see that bubbles of it were forming behind the white paint on the wall. Eventually the inevitable happened and the concrete started to break away leaving a nasty gap in what we called 'the concrete bulge'. It seemed that the chimney would have to be lined. Oh dear, an unexpected expense.

And yet more because we decided to have the 'fosse', the septic tank, emptied and a tanker arrived to suck it all out. It was driven by an elderly man who we later discovered was eighty-six years old. His wife arrived a few minutes later and, donning her pinafore, heaved the heavy pipes into position. Finally she dealt with the paper work after he had finished the job and departed. Not a subject to dwell on but a necessary aspect of not being on mains drainage. Once more, a fortuitous move it turned out to have been in the following year.

That wet weather on 19th March rapidly

improved and by the 23rd it was warm enough to have our lunch outside in front of the cabin but winter was still there in the background and by March 30th we had snow. Again it was very changeable and within a few days it was hot enough to be sitting outside the cabin again.

Our son Tim, his wife Sue and their son Alex were paying us their second visit and were keen to see the changes we had made since they first came two years earlier. They were very complimentary about what we had done and we were so glad that in their busy lives they had managed to visit us again. Tim, who is a keen cyclist and who has completed several arduous rides in England and in the French Alps and on Mont Ventoux in Provence, had brought his bike with him as had Alex and they went off on a tour of the villages and countryside nearby.

As far as Sue was concerned a trip to the well-known market at St Hilaire du Harcouët was a must for that visit. So on a cold, breezy but sunny day off we went. It was quite hard to find a parking space for all the world seemed to be at the market. The main square was packed with stalls selling a huge variety of things such as meat, fish, sausages, fruit and vegetables, local produce like honey and cider, cheeses of course, clothing, material and shoes. One man had an interesting stall showing how he restored chairs, so if you bought old chairs from the vide grenier or brocante you could take them to him and he would restore them for you. Useful to know.

The area which really attracted our attention was where the poultry was being sold. There were cages of hens, ducks and geese but most appealing of all were the tiny goslings, ducklings and fluffy yellow chicks. Sue was very keen to have chickens of her own in her garden in England and could hardly bear to tear herself away from these gorgeous balls of fluff.

Not long after they had gone home spring was in full swing again and once more the hedgerows were marked by the blossom of the wild cherry trees that we could see as we looked out from the garden across the valley and beyond. The verges of the lanes were burgeoning with wild flowers, bees were buzzing and birds were singing. It is a beautiful time of the year in the bocage country of small fields and sunken lanes here in the northern part of the Pay de La Loire in the Mayenne area.

Soon after our visitors had returned home we decided we really must get something done about the chimney. We called a builder in to view the situation and he confirmed our suspicions that the chimney would have to be lined. 'Pas de problem', no problem, he said. Little did we know!

However despite his lack of English and our struggling French it was agreed that a flexible stainless steel liner could be pushed up from the bottom or down from the top and that the men would come to do it in a few days. The flue from the wood burner was removed and we were ready for our new flue liner which would solve all out nasty, sticky tarry mess problems.

Or not, as it turned out because when the men arrived with the shiny new liner try as they might it couldn't be pushed up from the bottom or down from the top. The men got on the phone to their boss who came quickly from whatever job he was on to view the situation. After much head scratching it was decided that something was blocking the chimney and the only answer would be an outside flue. He would send us a 'devis', an estimate, in a few days.

We were not at all keen on an unsightly outside

flue and knew that it would be expensive. I think the builder must have been thinking along those lines too for he never did send the devis. We were wondering if we would have to abandon the idea of having a wood burner and just rely on electric heaters but we didn't want to do that at all. We loved sitting by our cheerful wood burner on chilly evenings.

So as John's thoughts were running along the lines of 'if the chimney is blocked what is blocking it?' mine were thinking about treasure or something more sinister left over from the Second World War. We'd had enough mess in the cottage with all the renovations but John tentatively suggested taking out a section of the plaster board in the bedroom and investigating the blockage from there.

So that is what he did and found a large space behind the plaster board on either side of the flue. Had we known how much space had been left between it and the outside wall of the cottage I think we might have utilised that space for wardrobes but it was too late for that now.

Fortunately he didn't discover anything sinister and there was no treasure. Shame! It was just that the flue narrowed thus preventing the flexible stainless steel liner from sliding through.

Nothing daunted John started to break into the flue and by carefully chipping away he widened it enough for the new liner to fit. He was on the phone to the builder again and once more the men came with the flexible flue and attempted to push it down the chimney. Success, thank goodness. I think the builder was pleased too for I'm sure he felt the same way as we did about an outside flue.

So the job was finished off around the time fires would be unnecessary anyway. We tried it out with a small one and all was well. What a relief, we could now look forward to cosy evenings watching the flickering flames of our 'poêle a bois' on the chilly nights of next autumn.

We ordered a tonne of gravel to top up the garden path and were amused when it arrived in the bucket of a digger. It was dumped in the parking area; using the wheelbarrow it was carted and tipped onto the path, then raked out level. It looked very smart when finished.

We also went to visit an interesting and colourful garden a few miles from here called Les Renaudies which is renowned for the magnificent rhododendrons in May. We have visited it several times and enjoy walking on the extensive lawns. The gardens contain some attractive and unusual trees and borders, filled with shrubs, perennials and annuals. There is a pond and a large ornamental waterwheel and a very interesting museum of rural life. At certain times of the year plants are for sale.

Another garden that we like very much is Le Jardin de La Pellerine situated on the road between Ernée and Fougères. It's a two hectare private garden looked after by the hardworking owners. It is similar in size to the garden we had at Larch Cottage which we opened under the National Garden Scheme but has many more delightful gardens-within-gardens and stunning flower borders with well thought out planting schemes. We particularly enjoy going there in June when the roses are at their best.

*La Pellerine*

We are also delighted with the progress our own garden has made since we had bought the cottage in February 2011. We had a blank canvas to work on with the garden which at first consisted of just a piece of rectangular grass and a border onto which all kinds of rubbish had been dumped. I cleared the old border and we planted shrubs and perennials, later there was the potager and then the grass bed which you have read about previously.

When we come back in March the daffodils are in full bloom, first of all the yellow ones and then my favourites, the scented white Narcissus poeticus. The fruit trees we planted are coming into blossom too; the pretty pink apple and creamy pear blossom, the white Mirabelle blossom and the pink apricot flowers add beauty and interest all their own.

Later, the tulips planted in the border the previous autumn are in flower while the perennials are gathering their strength for a magnificent show.

One of the first is the white and sweetly scented Hesperis matronalis, the sweet rocket much loved by butterflies and, to our delight, sometimes visited by very handsome Swallowtail butterflies.

The blue Iris sibirica flowers at the same time while the rest of the 'gang' are building up their foliage and waiting for their turn. I think the

most impressive of these are the Delphiniums 'Pacific Giants' which flower for weeks and when, after flowering, if completely cut down to the base of the plant will produce another magnificent show again in August.

Lupins, nepeta and hardy geraniums are also some of the early summer flowers while later there are roses, clematis, penstemons and hemerocallis and then for the final summer show we have rudbeckias, sedums and dahlias. I say final summer show but in fact this show goes on until well into October at which time we are thinking about tidying up the border and planting tulips for yet another magnificent show in the following spring.

The potager has done well too. In our first visit of the year it is something we are particularly keen to get started on. Near to Gorron there is an enterprising centre for people with learning difficulties where they grow plants for sale. There are several huge polytunnels and we go there to buy plants; lettuce, tomato, cucumber and courgettes. We have also bought roses, bedding plants and pelargoniums. They have a huge range and the quality is very good. Adjacent to the plant centre is a restaurant that employs these people and it is very popular at lunch time. Next door to that is a metal work centre where they also work.

So armed with our new plants we get busy in the potager and sow peas and beans as well. The soil is very fertile and we get good crops. The peas do very well and by staggering the planting we get two or three harvests. In June the strawberries start ripening. They are soft, sweet, succulent fruit well worth waiting for and very different from strawberries imported from Spain to our supermarkets during the winter. It amuses us to remember that the parent plants of the ones we have here in France were grown on our allotment in Chichester several years ago. In the autumn we have an excellent crop of raspberries.

At either end of the potager we have flowers both for their beauty and to attract pollinators to the garden. At the far end we have a band of semi-wild flowers which also include poppies and Love-in-the-Mist. At the cottage end we have bright dahlias and pot marigolds. We think the garden looks very attractive and we often see walkers who go past the cottage stopping to admire the garden.

This is a quiet backwater of France away from the tourist hot spots of Provence, the Dordogne and the Cote d'Azur. The delights of the Loire Valley are just over two hours' drive away to the south and it is a similar distance to the Vendée. The Normandy beaches are also two hours' drive away to the north with Mont St Michel, Dinard and St Malo only slightly more and the western coast of Brittany is within easy reach. The TGV, Train Grande Vitesse, reaches Paris in two hours from Laval. So it's all going on out there and this area is easily bypassed, so it's quiet and property prices are low. But that doesn't mean that life here has to be dull. If you want social activity it's there in terms of the EuroMayenne society, boules games, choirs, vide greniers, markets, eating out and going to see places. If you just want to sit in your garden with a glass of wine looking at the view, that's alright too.

When friends visited in June 2013 we went to the lovely old town of Vitré. Our friend is a keen cyclist and highly knowledgeable about all things to do with the cycling world. The following week the Tour de France was passing through this area so the journey to Vitré was considerably enlivened by his excitement about the race and the cyclists participating, including Bradley Wiggins who had come first the previous year. Now in 2013 Chris Froome was the favourite and we were told all about his chances for winning the race which he subsequently succeeded in doing.

"Surely you are going to see it?" our friend asked.

"Well, actually no." we replied.

"Oh how could you miss such an exciting event?" And so on.

Eventually we arrived in Vitré which is one of the best preserved cities in Brittany with its timber framed houses, old streets, chateau, ramparts and a religious heritage.

The site had been occupied in Gallo-Roman times and in the year 1000 Geoffrey 1, Duke of Brittany gave feudal powers to Riwallon Le Vicaire who was given the responsibility of keeping this strategic area as a buffer zone

known as the Marches of Brittany rather like the Welsh Marches. At first there was a small wooden motte and bailey castle; in 1070 a stone castle was built, certain parts of which can still be seen today.

In the 13th century it was enlarged and given strong towers and curtain walls. The old town and the church of Notre-Dame were surrounded by fortified ramparts and ditches and thus it became a traditional medieval city.

During the Middle Ages many half-timbered houses and private mansions were built within the walls and a network of narrow streets and lanes developed. As with other medieval towns, streets gained their names from the trades practised there.

Vitré was a prosperous city from the 15<sup>th</sup> century with a peak in the 16<sup>th</sup> century when its hemp fabric was sold throughout Europe.

When Henry the Fourth passed through the

city in 1598 he was struck by the opulence of the middle-class merchants and declared that if he were not the King of France he would like to be a middle-class man of Vitré.

At one time the city was besieged by the English; it seems to have been a stalemate situation for after a year or two the inhabitants of Vitré simply paid the besiegers to go back home. In the 17th century the barons of Vitré flocked to the Court of Versailles and the city became a quiet place.

We spent a very enjoyable time wandering around the old streets and visiting the chateau.

Our visit was concluded with lunch sitting outside at the Auberge du Chateau in the warm sunshine.

And then on the way back to the cottage we were given a quiz about the Tour de France. I'm afraid we didn't get a very high score. I can tell you that often its route is over stunning scenery in the Alps and the Pyrenees but the intricacies of the Tour de France are quite beyond me. I hear it's coming much closer to the cottage on its way to Fougères in 2015, so maybe I shall feel I must go and have a look as the 'caravan' goes by. I understand the competitors are here one minute and gone a few seconds later, it's all over in a flash!

\*\*\*\*\*\*

In July we went to Dinard on Brittany's Côte d'Émeraude finding when we arrived that it was market day so there was not a parking space to be found anywhere. Eventually we found somewhere by a campsite at Port Blanc on the outskirts of the town and had an enjoyable walk back along the coast path from where we were able see the off shore islands and to admire the splendid cliff top villas built by British and American aristocrats in the late 19th century during the French Belle Époque.

At that time it was popular as a summer resort but in the 1930s the Jet Set started to prefer the Côte d'Azur. There are views of St Malo across the River Rance, well known for its tidal power station opened in 1966.

I thought Dinard was a very attractive place with architecturally interesting buildings, sea views and wide sandy beaches. John had memories of taking a school party there in 1971; he identified the hotel in which he had stayed with a group of twelve sixth form students, commenting that it looked somewhat more stylish than formerly.

Footsore and weary after several hours wandering round sightseeing we were glad to be able to get a taxi to take us back to where we had parked the car.

\*\*\*\*\*\*

Now that the renovations on the cottage were completed we enjoyed being tourists from time to time and our summer of sightseeing continued with a visit to Le Mans about seventy miles away from the cottage. We were not going to the race track as the medieval centre of the city was our goal that day. Once again initially parking was a problem but this time it was due to the chaos caused by new tram lines being laid in the centre of the town and extensive modernisation of the area in front of the cathedral. I'm sure it will look wonderful when it is all finished.

Having eventually found a spacious underground car park we emerged into the open air again but were completely disorientated. I asked a woman with a baby in a pushchair where the medieval centre of Le Mans was and she said we were to follow her as she was on her way home to lunch. She was a fast walker and we charged after her through the streets so we got there in double quick time.

It's quite amazing that in such a large and busy city there should be such a charming old centre. After visiting the cathedral we had lunch at a restaurant in one of the medieval streets and then went to have a look at the Roman walls built to surround the town in the third century. Today they are some of the most complete Gallo Roman city walls to survive.

Our walk back to the car was taken at a more leisurely pace and we had time to look around. I bought a navy and red silk scarf and whenever I wear it I remember our day in Le Mans.

\*\*\*\*\*\*

On a very hot day in September 2013 we visited Le Mont St Michel. Since the spring of the previous year a huge new car park had been opened some distance away from the Mont. Visitors now have the choice of riding on the Shuttle bus or walking across the marshes to the rocky islet. Or a third option is available

which is to go on the 'Maringote', a horse
drawn shuttle. Adjacent to the car park is a
well-appointed information centre.

This is all part of a wide reaching scheme to
restore the area to its maritime character. Over
the years with land reclamation and the
creation of the causeway to the mainland,
sediment has built up and the sea has been
pushed further away. It has now been decided
to use the natural power of the tide and the
River Couesnon to restore it. A dam and a
hydraulic system on the river is central to this
work. Without a large car park at its base the
Mont now looks more as it must have looked
in earlier times or at least it will when the work

is completed later this year. From high up on the Mont you can get a good idea of what it is hoped to achieve. The new road layout with the construction of a long low level bridge and the removal of the causeway will increase the ability of the river and tide to scour away sandbanks and sediment. The Mont will once again become a rocky islet separate from the mainland.

You need strong lungs and a good pair of legs to enjoy your visit to the Mont as there are steep streets and many steps. The streets are thronged with tourists of all nationalities keen to visit this World Heritage site. As you climb through the narrow streets and up the steep steps forever twisting and turning upwards you get glimpses between buildings and roof tops of the sea and the marshland spread out below. Eventually, nearer to the top the view of the surrounding sea and marshes is stunning in its beauty. This is an extraordinary place with buildings clinging to the rock and crowned by the Abbey. Hermit monks lived here from the sixth century but the solitude they found is a far cry from the bustling tourism of today.

Before the causeway was built pilgrims faced a perilous journey across the bay with the dangers of quicksand, swirling mist and a tide that could race in very quickly and surround the unwary traveller. The pilgrims kept their eyes on the spire of the Abbey of Mont St Michel surmounted by the gilded statue of St Michel and hoped he would protect them.

After negotiating the narrow bustling streets lined with gift shops selling a wide variety of goods and mementoes, and passing many eateries, we continued upwards and finally entered the abbey. During the time of the French Revolution and Empire it was turned into a prison; it was restored before the end of the 19th century. Not to be missed is the giant tread-wheel once powered by six prisoners to haul two ton loads of stone up from the landing point below. The Abbey is vast and awe inspiring and I found it a little frightening too and was glad to escape outside into the sunshine again.

Back at the cottage we eat our meals by the cabin as often as the weather permits. We love to sit there looking at our garden and also at the wonderful far reaching views over the valley and beyond.

We are glad to see that many bees and butterflies come to visit our flowers. Sparrow hawks swoop across the valley and buzzards hover overhead or spiral up into the sky as their plaintive cries echo round the valley below. Green woodpeckers laugh at us as they fly away and lesser Spotted Woodpeckers bore into our hazel tree, itself plundered for nuts by red squirrels in the autumn. We see tree creepers, blue tits, chaffinches, bats and many other birds. Crows shout raucously and in spring and summer blackbirds proclaim their territorial rights by singing loudly from a roof or tree top. In early summer the swallows arrive and in the evenings swoop and swirl above the garden catching insects. In the autumn they gather on the telephone wires twittering about when they should leave and then suddenly they rise as one and they are off leaving the younger birds to follow on later. These are the miracles of migration.

When they go we know summer has ended. If we are lucky, and we often are, we have a while longer to enjoy a glass of wine in sunny moments by the cabin and watch the end of the harvest being gathered in. Several hay crops each year are taken from the field across the lane which has been sown with clover to enrich it. During the summer we watch the barley and then the wheat being harvested and then last of all it is the tall maize which in one season has grown to eight feet high. When that goes it is as if a forest has been cut down. Where there was a field of tall maize yesterday, today it has gone and heavily loaded trailers take it from the fields and along the narrow lanes.

Whereas years ago you would see the maize cobs drying in racks for animal feed, today the whole plant is minced up as it is harvested, then stored and used for animal fodder.

Across the valley there is an ever-changing patchwork of colours as month by month fields are ploughed, crops are planted, grow and ripen and then finally they are harvested.

The farmers work incredibly hard and when bad weather is forecast there is a tremendous effort to work all the hours God sends to get the work done or the harvest in. As I write we are at the end of weeks of dry weather and it is raining at last but the maize harvest has only just started so I'm afraid that for this year they won't be getting it in while it is dry.

I mentioned earlier that when John severely pruned some trees at the end of the garden in December 2011 I had helped to heave them out of the way resulting in a back problem that refused to go away. Eventually at the beginning of 2014 I went to a physiotherapist in Chichester who told me that one hip was nearly an inch higher than the other one. She set to work on me assuring me that it was 'fixable'.

'Thank goodness for that,' I thought but what I didn't realise at first was that in the year since I had first upset my hips my shoulders had tried to compensate for uneven hips by becoming unbalanced themselves. As the physiotherapist straightened up my hips so all my shoulder and then arm muscles started to shift back again and that was very painful indeed. I was unable to walk without pain and for a while was even unable to dress myself. Slowly, very slowly the situation improved. Had I been at home all the time the physio would have been able to continue working on me but after six weeks of treatment it was time to come back to France.

So I continued with the exercises and, with the occasional physio treatment during our short visits home, the situation improved slowly but far too slowly for my liking. I decided that I would like to find a physio in France who could continue the good work. What I hadn't been aware of was that, unlike at home in England, I had to visit the doctor first in order to be able to arrange that. So first thing one Monday morning I arranged an appointment (a 'rendezvous') at the local surgery and requested an English speaking doctor 's'il vous plait si c'est possible'. And yes it was possible to see an English speaking doctor and surprisingly I was able to see her on the same day. I went back that afternoon and waited for quite a while in the waiting room. Eventually she saw me and spent forty minutes with me. I felt sorry for those still in the waiting room. However when I explained about my hip problem she gave me a good going over, said I should have a blood test and an X-ray and then go to see her with the results.

The blood test was done the next day at a walk in surgery in the main street of Gorron, no appointment necessary and I only waited about ten minutes. I was told to pick up the results at the pharmacy two days later. Then we went to Mayenne to find out where the X-ray clinic was and made an appointment; another surprise, it would be done the next day.

So the following day we went back to Mayenne. I was thoroughly X-rayed and then told to wait a few minutes and the radiologist would see me. My husband was with me when I saw this charming man who spoke excellent English and put the X-rays up on a screen in order to discuss the results with us. It was good to be told that my hips were level again. So the next day I picked up my blood test results and the following day, Friday, I went back to see the doctor. The blood tests showed that I had inflammation, well that was the pain in my shoulders which were taking their time over catching up with my nicely level hips so no physiotherapy was needed after all. My physio in the UK had been right, it was fixable.

So there we were, five days from start to finish. How long would all that take in England? In France we paid for each stage as we went along. Twenty-three euros for the doctor's appointment, two or three euros for the nurse to take a blood sample, about ninety euros for the X-rays and consultation with the radiologist, six euros for the lab work on my blood and another twenty-three euros to see the doctor again. At each place I was given a form to fill in which eventually, after our return home, was sent to the Overseas Healthcare Team at the Department for Work and Pensions in Washington, Tyne and Wear in the north of England.

A few weeks later I received a cheque for the full amount that I had spent. In France I had been given prompt efficient service for which ultimately I had not had to pay a penny. I could not have been more impressed.

My hip and shoulder problems have been very slow to get better but my physio insists it is fixable so I must be patient and my problems have made me much more appreciative of my generally good health and the fact that I will get better. So I am thankful.

Also there has been a silver lining to this situation because my inactivity has made it possible to write my second book **'The Flowers in my Bouquet'** and get it published and to start on this, my third book. And next summer, since I am fixable, I hope very much to have been finally 'fixed' and to be able to enjoy walking again. Well if not......Book Four I suppose!

An enjoyable event each year is the annual Bastille Day celebration throughout France on the fourteenth of July. In 2014 in the evening we joined with a group of sixteen friends to have a meal at a restaurant adjacent to the Chateau in Mayenne, set high above the river.

At eleven o'clock we all went out onto the terrace of the restaurant overlooking the river. Down below were the old 'quais' where boats had once unloaded their cargoes. There and on the two bridges were crowds of people who had come to see the fireworks. From eleven o'clock for half an hour there was an incredible spectacle of colour and noise. It was continuous and it was amazing. The fireworks had been set up on three barges moored in the river and we had a splendid view from our vantage point.

In July there was a spell of hot dry weather, perfect for excursions such as the one we made to the lake at Selle de Gué where we had a picnic overlooking the sparkling water. On another occasion when we had been there we had walked all the way round the lake and had seen a group of school children having a sailing lesson. It was a pleasure to see them wearing life jackets and bobbing about in tiny boats.

On another very hot day we went to the Roman town of Jublains. There we explored the remains of a huge fortress, the amphitheatre and the baths discovered under the church. A museum on the site is full of interest. Named Noviodunum in Roman times Jublains was an administrative centre for this region of Gaul and had been the capital of the ancient Gallic tribe of Diablintes.

*Photo on next page*

Now thought to have been a fortified granary depot for the area it may also have been important on the trade route between Italy and Britain. One can imagine the Roman soldiers patrolling Hadrian's Wall in the north of England eating figs and olive oil and drinking wine from Italy that had travelled through France and Noviodunum on their way north from the sunny south to the grey and misty Northumberland landscape.

Then August came round again and it was time to go home for a couple of weeks to be with the family and friends and this year to celebrate our Golden Wedding We have been very blessed with a long and happy marriage and with two wonderful sons and their families. It's always lovely to meet up with them. The eldest grandchild left university two years ago; our granddaughter has left school and the younger grandson has just two more years to go at school. The years go so fast and it's important to make the most of life.

\*\*\*\*\*\*

When we were back at the cottage for our autumn visit the trees were just beginning to turn but the poplars had lost their leaves some time ago possibly because it was so dry all through September. The sweet chestnuts were ripe and falling off the trees in large quantities. Trixie dislikes walking on this prickly carpet but local people collect big bags full of them. They are definitely slow food. I must make an effort with them next year as people keep telling me how good they are and free of course!

We had many misty mornings when gradually, as the mist cleared, the hidden view re-emerged and then the sun came out and the dew covered cobwebs sparkled in the sunshine. The lawn was wet with diamond droplets far into the day. By evening when it was getting chilly there was a hint of wood smoke in the air and plumes of smoke curled upwards from Le Bas Pin farm below us and from cottage chimneys round and about including ours.

A degree of panic set in when everyone round here had a letter to say it was time to have their fosse septique inspected. People are concerned that if their fosse doesn't pass the test they will have to spend four to five thousand euros having a new one installed. Yes, well you can understand that can't you? When we came here there was nothing visible above ground so John dug down, found where our fosse was and made sure the inspection covers were on the surface and visible. But we had no paper work about it and on application to the Mairie they didn't either. We were worried in case we had to dig down to discover where the trenches are that lead the water away from it.

Inspection morning arrived and the technician who came couldn't have been more helpful.

His name was Monsieur Grande and he spoke English which was a big help. He had a good look at our fosse. Thank goodness John had raised those inspection covers. He said the drainage trenches were working as the level in the fosse was where it should be. He looked at the fruit trees we had planted and said that as the roots of fruit trees didn't go particularly deep they wouldn't interfere with the drains. The ventilation pipe John had put in also met with his approval although he said a different kind of 'hat' on it might be more effective.

Then he came inside to fill in the paper work. He said that to maintain our fosse in good working order it should be fed with a pot of yogurt every fortnight. So all was well, no further expense. That was a huge relief. He also taught us a new word....the French for paper clip is 'trombone'. The song 'Seventy six paper clips' wouldn't have the same...je ne sais quoi....would it?

We had a hornets nest in one of our chimneys during the autumn and watched them for several weeks flying in and out. Our tolerance faded when we found them hovering outside our only door, the menacing angry buzzing of their wings discouraging entry or exit. Neither was I enamoured to see – and hear – the occasional hornet hovering outside the shower room window whilst I had my shower! Finally we felt we must do something about getting them exterminated so Monsieur Ribot came to destroy the nest. Although when he arrived he was wearing shorts we were relieved to see that he wore full protective clothing when he climbed up the ladder and started to spray his insecticide into the chimney.

The hornets got quite cross about that, naturally, but soon the activity died down.

However when we went inside, having been watching proceedings from a safe point in the garden, we found that about sixty of them had found their way inside through a small space in the chimney. The poor dog was most concerned and had retreated into a corner while she watched the hornets in their death throes. Monsieur Ribot came in and asked for the 'aspirateur', the vacuum cleaner, which he used to suck up the bodies even looking under cushions to make sure he had found them all. We were most impressed.

This had been interesting and was yet another of the experiences to add to those of living in France. Now we no longer had to worry about the hornets coming inside and one of us or the dog getting stung. We felt liberated. The hornets were beyond feeling anything.

Soon it was time to go home again and we went on the ferry to Portsmouth. I used to have a real phobia about going on the ferry. When we lived in Kent and before the Channel Tunnel was built we had some quite rough crossings between Dover and Calais. My fear of going on the boat continued until this year. After the Tunnel was opened in 1994 it was very easy to use that route and we got used to driving onto the train with the caravan we owned at the time.

However since moving to West Sussex going through the Tunnel has meant turning away from the ferry port at Portsmouth only twenty minutes away from home and driving for two hours along some of the most congested roads in the UK before going through the Tunnel and onto the quieter roads in France. We will still do that if the sea is rough but having discovered an internet site called 'Passage Weather' we can find out what the sea state will be up to a week ahead and can plan our trip accordingly and go from Portsmouth to Caen with only two hours driving once we get into France. The total journey time whether we go by ferry from Portsmouth or drive through Kent to the Tunnel is almost exactly the same, about nine hours, but six hours relaxing in a cabin on the boat is much less stressful than spending those extra hours on the road.

So for the week before it is time to go home we frequently look at 'Passage Weather' and hope to be able to choose a day when the sea is calm. Otherwise we will travel on a Sunday when there are virtually no lorries on the French roads and driving is a pleasure. But as soon as we get back on the English motorways it is a different matter altogether.

Sundays are altogether quieter in France than in England. What with no lorries on the roads and no supermarkets open in the smaller towns it is Sunday as it used to be in England. Families get together and enjoy long relaxed meals and talk to each other or go out together for a barbecue on the beach or in the countryside. No wonder so many of us are opting to live in the more relaxed atmosphere of France even, as in our case, when we do it for only half of the year.

\*\*\*\*\*\*\*\*\*\*\*\*\*\*

*Sadly, since the preparation of this book, the learning difficulties centre near Gorron has closed due to economic problems*

# Bon Appétit
## Agneau Pré-Salé
## (Lamb raised on the salt marshes)

Sheep have been raised for centuries on the salt marshes surrounding Mont St Michel. Their diet of plants that thrive in those conditions gives a subtle and much sought after flavour to the spring lamb. What a delicious meal this would be for your Easter Sunday feast. It seems that the monks from the Abbey of Mont St Michel had the right to take one lamb from nearby flocks so they too were feasting on pré-salé lamb.

For six to eight people you will need a 2kg joint of lamb.

100g of salted butter

Fresh thyme

Some cloves of garlic

Rosemary

Salt and pepper

Coat the lamb with softened butter combined with chopped thyme and freshly ground black pepper.

Make incisions in the flesh with a sharp knife and insert slivers of garlic. Lay sprays of fresh rosemary across the top of the joint.

Place the meat in a roasting tin with a cupful of water and roast in a pre-heated hot oven, 180°-190°C for between forty minutes and an hour and baste it once or twice while it is cooking.

After the meat comes out of the oven rest it in a warm place for twenty minutes while you add wine or/and water to the pan juices to make a gravy. Allow to bubble. Strain before using as bits of rosemary are not good in gravy. That twenty minutes will give you time to roast par-boiled potatoes that have been tossed in olive oil. Samphire would be an interesting accompaniment to this or buttered spring cabbage.

*******

# Chapter Eleven
## Who lived here in the Past?

I love this place high up above the valley. Opposite to us is a hay field sloping down to the farm of Le Bas Pin and then a further slope down to the river. The river with its water mills from times past; the river and nearby footpaths used for hundreds, maybe thousands of years by people who lived in this valley from as long ago as the Stone Age or before, who hunted in these woods as Le Chasse does today but obviously not with orange hi-viz jackets, camouflage clothing and carrying guns.

These Stone Age hunter gatherers were naked or had an animal skin tied round their bodies, with a clutch of flint tipped arrows as they stalked their prey. They moved silently from tree to tree, from rock to rock as they kept their eye on their quarry in this valley. No easy trip to Super U for them to pick a packet of meat off the shelf and certainly no fast food apart from the odd blackberry. No, if they wanted to eat, if they wanted to feed their families they had to be skilful hunters. It was initially a slow and well thought out process and not always successful for when their prey got away the people went hungry.

Here in Europe they would have hunted for mammoths, mastodons, aurochs, deer and bears and in the River Colmont they would have found fish. I can imagine that a group of hunters would manage to corral an animal into one of the gorges along the valley and then to converge on it from all directions and go in for the kill. It must have been very dangerous for the hunters but vital for their survival.

In between hunts they would live on nuts and berries but when they had made a kill they would have carried the animal back to their cave or simple shelter and there would have been feasting in their tribe as they shared out the spoils. These people were hunter gatherers and moved from place to place. They were not farmers then but gradually made clearings in the forest and simple wattle and daub dwellings were built; they started to rear animals and grow crops. They gradually settled down and became farmers.

I think of this collection of dwellings here at La Vesquerie as a farm hamlet and have come across records of it once being known as the village of La Vesquerie, sometimes known as La Vequerie or La Vaquerie. We have often wondered how to pronounce the name Vesquerie, sounding the 's' or leaving it silent. We have come across both ways of saying it among the locals.

And we have often wondered what it means. Putting Vaquerie into the French dictionary on my iPad I find that 'vaquer à ses occupations' means to go about one's business. Could people in the far distant past have seen the people here as people busily tending their land and animals. Could it have meant 'the busy place'? Just a thought.

So in thinking about who these people were who lived at La Vesquerie in the past I look for clues. Among this group of buildings only three are occupied now but there are other buildings. Were they once lived in I wonder? Who was it who tied his horse to the iron ring set in the wall of a ruin just up the yard? Who were the people who sat round the fire in the ruined cottage where you can just see the outlines of a large fireplace such as there must once have been in this cottage?

And who were the people who used the lavoir just along the lane where a spring trickles water into a concrete trough that someone made maybe two hundred years ago; the spring that centuries ago, when there was more water around, carved out a small valley that is now wooded and leads down to join the River Colmont near to Le Bas Pin? They must have been the women from the village of La Vesquerie and that means it goes back over two hundred years. I imagine they came in twos and threes and had a good chatter while they did their laundry. There is a lavoir in every village around here some of them are roofed over to shelter the women from the rain or the sun. The nearest one in Brecé is just round the corner from La Fontaine again making use of a stream.

And what about the piles of stones dotted

around in nearby fields? Were they once homes? We certainly know of one that was as we went to look at it before some of the stone was taken away for renovating a building elsewhere. The doorway, windows and roof were clearly visible but now it is just a pile of stones like the others. I suspect they were once simple stone dwellings that, once unlived in, fell into ruin. These dwellings may have had low stone walls topped by a roof of stout branches, overlaid with turf to keep out the worst of the weather. I think the farmers added to the piles of stones when they removed stones from the fields and then in the mists of time people forgot that there had ever been a dwelling there.

But not only can the stone be reused for renovating other buildings. We have seen it being used to put down in gateways to limit the amount of mud churned up by heavy farm machinery. Just now, as I write with the maize harvest in full swing, stone has been taken from our nearest heap of stones to a place lower down the lane where the machinery for gathering the maize later today or tomorrow will be going over it. Our quiet lane will be for a short time a busy and noisy place.

With the removal of nearly half of this pile of stones we can see the ground and there is bed rock which would have a made a solid foundation for the house that we believe was there. There are some large chunks of stone that could easily have been corner stones. So maybe these other half dozen or so piles of stones nearby met the same fate and were once small houses. Maybe stone from them was even used for these buildings at La Vesquerie.

Perhaps an archaeological survey would find evidence of post holes denoting that there might have been earlier simple wattle and daub type houses but of course there is no visible evidence to support this idea. For the last two or three hundred years at least local stone was used for the buildings here but further north in Normandy some of the buildings are 'colombage', that is a timber frame with something akin to wattle and daub filling in the spaces, much like the black and white timbered houses in for example Herefordshire in

England.

So there were too many 'maybes'. It was time to look for firm evidence of what had happened here in the past. With a lot of experience behind me in searching for my family's genealogy for my book **'The Flowers in my Bouquet'** I knew the next step was to find local archives. Mayenne Archives are on-line and free. Here at my desk in our tiny cottage at La Vesquerie the past gradually began to unfold.

Obviously I am particularly interested in what happened here and I don't imagine that you will totally share my interest but what follows shows what you can do if you want to find out more about where you live. If you don't, you have the option of skipping the next bit.

Here are just some of the records I searched:-

The census records, 'les recensements de population,' from 1836 every five years through to 1911;

Parish registers for Brecé dating from the sixteenth century until 1902.

Plans du Cadastre Napoléon, maps dating from 1833.

The Mongraphie Communales.

I also found the Cassini maps on line.

And I went to the library and came across the Diaries of l'Abbé Angot.

A quick glance at the Parish registers showed me they were an exact photographic copy of the originals even down to rodent and water damage that had occurred to some of them; often flowery and indecipherable handwriting of all sizes with blots and splodges and of course in French. At the time I didn't feel my French was up to wading through page after page of that.

******

*Brecé church interior*

*Brecé church exterior*

The Monographies Communales were fascinating records of each canton written in 1899 by the teachers of the Mayenne Department and presented at the Universal Exhibition, a World Fair, held in Paris in 1900 for several months to celebrate the achievements of the last century and the hopes for the next. I would certainly be coming back to that and looking at it in detail.

The Plans Cadastres were maps made of each region in France in 1833 showing dwellings, field boundaries and roads existing at the time. Very useful for my research here as the map for this area showed the buildings of the time at La Vesquerie plus outlines of small plots close to them which I imagine were people's potagers. It shows field boundaries as well.

But at first it was the census figures, 'recensements de population', to which I turned in more detail. Who exactly had lived here, where had they come from, what jobs did they do, how old were they?

The first census in 1836 gave a list of twenty people living in the various cottages at La Vesquerie but unfortunately neither in this census nor any of the others was there any indication of who lived in which property so I have never been able to discover for certainty who lived in our cottage.

Here in 1836 lived the families of Trihan, Derrenne, Aubert and Derrieux with the Derrieux family being the only one to have a servant. The wives were given using their maiden names which was later helpful in trying to trace family links. By tying these names in with later research I could see that at least four of these people had been born before the

French Revolution and one in that year. They were Perrine Trihan, an unmarried woman born in 1751 and the oldest person in the settlement. At eighty-five she must have had a strong constitution to survive the rigours of her times. Jean Derrenne was born in 1767, Jeanine Derrenne in 1765 and Madeline Garnier, propriétaire, widow of François Derrieux, in 1777. René Aubert was born in the actual year of the Revolution. So Madeline Garnier was the owner of the property. I suspect that means all the houses here. Does that mean she lived in the one house here that is larger than the others and has a bread oven?

None of this information told me when these houses were built. That is what I really wanted to know. For that I needed to start trying to decipher those parish records to see if I could find out the date of the first person to be born here. But that would have to wait until I felt brave enough to try to decipher all that squiggly writing.

In the 1841 census in the 'village de la Vesquerie' the families were listed by households and there were five of them. The previous families had been joined by the Cruchét family and André Cruchét's wife, a spinner, was Marie Julienne Trihan. André Cruchét was a 'journalier', a worker hired out on a daily basis. Madeline Garnier's son Cesar Derrieux, a farmer, was the owner of the property now. Michel Trihan, a widower, his son Pierre and another Michel Trihan, a married man, were 'sabotiers' that is clog makers. Perrine and Prudence Trihan, daughters of Michel the widower were 'fileuses', spinners as were Louise Lochu wife of Michel Trihan and Renée Fauveau, wife of René Aubert, a mason. Spinning was carried on in the home and I can imagine that the spinners gathered together and chatted while they spun the wool or flax. Clog making would have been quite messy with wood shavings and lumps of wood scattered around so they would have had a building where that activity could take place. At the gardens of Les Renaudies a model workshop has been set up in their museum where one can see the process of clog making. Once again, like the local stone being used for building, the 'sabotiers' were using a commodity of which there was an abundance locally.

*(Photos below, reconstructed sabotiers' workshop)*

In 1846 there were only four households here

in the 'hameau', hamlet, of la Vesquerie. Two of the men, including Cesar Derrieux, were farmers and two were clog makers. No spinning seems to have been going on then. Seven of the seventeen inhabitants were under twenty years of age.

In 1851 there were five households here consisting of a total of twenty-three people. Madeline's daughter Constance, born in 1819, had married Antoine François Gerard in 1842 and was missing from the 1846 census but by 1851 she was back with her daughter Marie Gerard born in 1848 but without her husband. Madeline's son Cesar was the only farmer at that time. René Aubert was a mason as was his son François and as Brecé was growing by now they must have had plenty of work. Four of the men were clog makers and all came from the two Trihan families that lived here. Anne Lochu and Virginé Aubert, daughter of René the mason were spinners. Eight people were aged under twenty.

In 1856 twenty-one people were living here in five households. At seventy-nine Madeline

Garnier was entered as a farmer and owner of the property. Her daughter Constance was also a farmer and her son Cesar now aged forty-eight would also have helped with the farming. The widow Anne Heuveline aged sixty-three was also entered as a farmer and property owner. It's interesting that this name should crop up here because in my later research of the parish records the name Heuveline occurred time after time from the 1700s onward and there are still Heuvelines in Brecé today as 'Travaux Publics', Public Works Contractors.

In 1856 there were two clog makers, Pierre Trihan aged forty-four and his wife Marie Buas aged thirty-two. The only spinner was Anne Lochu aged seventy, who was also a property owner. There were eleven people under twenty at this time.

In 1861 the Derrieux family was still going strong with Cesar now seemingly the head of the house and still farming. Constance Derrieux is recorded as being the wife of Antoine Gerard but where was he? Marie, her daughter, was now thirteen and Madeline was eighty-three. Some members of the Trihan family were still here but a newcomer on the block was Benoist Voisin, a carpenter who was a widower aged seventy. Living with him were Jeanne, his unmarried sister aged sixty, his son Auguste aged forty and his daughter Jeanne aged thirty-eight.

In 1866 there were five households and still the Derrieux family was here but Madeline at eighty-nine was 'grabotaire', bed-ridden; poor old lady.

There are several new names but Benoist Voisin, a widower is still a carpenter. He had married Perrine Jeanne Trihan at Brecé in 1813. Frederic Lochu aged forty-four was a 'courtier de bestiuex', an animal keeper. Lochu is a name that crops up in the parish register many times.

In the 1872 census Constance Derrieux at fifty-three is the only one of the Derrieux family still here. Presumably Madeline had died by now and maybe her granddaughter was married. The parish records show that Cesar died on the

19th November 1867 when he was fifty-nine. Another inhabitant was Julian Jean Lair, a journalier. His daughter Thérèse was lame but she was a spinner and another daughter Célestine was a 'tisserand', a weaver. The name Lair can still be seen in this area. Arsène Baudouin is on this census and also the following seven. He was a gravedigger in Brecé cemetery.

1876 is the last census on which Constance Derrieux appears at La Vesquerie; she was fifty-seven years old, a widow and lame.

From 1876 until 1911 there were five or six households here at each census so it must have been a busy place and the occupation of 'farmer' continues to feature as does spinning and weaving but clog making seems to have died out here at any rate. From 1901 the name of the employer or place of work was also added to the census information and thus the names Lelandais, Chopin and Guesson occur. Some people worked for themselves and 'patron' is entered for them.

In the 1906 census the place of birth has been

added if they were not born in Brecé although it seems that most of them were. The few that were born elsewhere came from the nearby villages of St Aubin Fosse Louvain, Le Pas and Colombier du Plessis. We can see the spire of Colombier du Plessis church from here about four miles away to the west. People didn't move very far away from their roots and we find even today that some people here have not travelled very far away from this immediate vicinity.

I was fascinated by the Derrieux family partly because they were here at La Vesquerie for so many years and also because the name Derrieux has been carved in stone on two of the houses in the village. Were they important people in some way I wondered?

In l'Abbé Angot's writings there is a mention of a François Derrieux being a delegate to a Provincial Assembly in 1799 to which, with Louis Lemarchand, the mayor, and François Pays, he took the parish records. This was ten years after the Revolution.

As can be seen later some of the Derrieux

family over the years were merchants in Brecé so, yes, I think they were people of standing in the community.

It was now time to go back to the flowery handwriting in the parish records to see if I could decipher anything which would tell me more about the Derrieux family and when La Vesquerie occurred for the first time in the records.

The earliest I have found so far is when in 1806 Pierre Lepelerin living at La Vequerie [*sic*] was a witness at the marriage of Hélène Derrieux, daughter of Michel Derrieux, a merchant who lived at Le Bas Pin which is just a field away down the hill from La Vesquerie. Every time I go out of the door I look down to the roof tops of Le Bas Pin. Julian Derrieux, merchant in Brecé was also a witness to that marriage. Hélène's son Mathieu was born the same year but Hélène died aged twenty-two quite probably in childbirth or soon afterwards. It's sad to think of such a tragedy occurring just at the bottom of the hill so close at hand.

In the same year, 1806, another Mathieu

Derrieux was living at La Vequerie when his fourteen year old daughter Renée died. I'm sure there was a connection between the Derrieux family at Le Bas Pin and the Derrieux family at La Vequerie. Maybe Mathieu and Michel were brothers and poor Hélène named her son after her uncle. The Derrieux family like many others named their descendants after fathers, uncles and grandparents.

In 1807 La Vequerie was mentioned when Mathieu Derrieux died there aged about sixty. He had been born at Brecé and was the son of another Mathieu Derrieux.

In 1808 there was a death at La Vequerie when Aimée Sophie Lepelerin died. She was the daughter of Pierre Lepelerin a tailor aged fifty, the same man who had been a witness at the marriage of Hélène Derrieux. And this same year Felicité Lepelerin died.

Pierre Lepelerin was a witness at the baptism of Michel Derrieux in 1808, son of René Derrieux of La Planchoterrie. La Planchoterrie is a farm on the other side of the valley above L'Ecluse. Another witness was Michel

Derrieux, 32, a carpenter living at La Monardière. This witness and his wife Magdalene Poirier had a daughter the same year. She was called Françoise Michelle Renée and the witness to her baptism was François Derrieux, 34, who lived in the village of Brecé and was the husband of Madeline Garnier. Madeline Garnier would later be living at La Vesquerie. Her husband François died in 1826 at La Vesquerie so sometime between the birth of Constance in 1818 recorded as being born in Brecé, and the death of François in 1826 the family moved to La Vesquerie.

Living in Brecé in 1808 was Julian Derrieux, mentioned above, a merchant aged 24, who was married to Renée Gabrielle Leroy. When their daughter Renée Gabrielle Françoise was baptised Michel Derrieux aged 64 was a witness. He was also a merchant living in Brecé.

So some members of the Derrieux family were merchants in Brecé where Michel was born in 1744 and Julian was born in 1784.

I discovered that Madeline Garnier was born in

Colombier du Plessis in 1777 and she married François Derrieux in Gorron in about 1800. They had at least five children, all born in Brecé. They were Victor François 1803, Benjamine Alexandre, 1806 and Romain 1806-1810, Cesar 1808-1867, Sergey Jean Victor 1808, and Constance in 1818 but none of them appear to have been born at La Vesquerie. So they can't have moved there when Mathieu Derrieux died there aged sixty in 1807. Presumably another Derrieux went there first.

In 1810 René Derrieux living at La Planchoterrie with his wife Marie Travigné had a daughter, Marie Magdelaine.

Also in 1810 another René Derrieux, aged 36, who lived at Le Vergeot died. Le Vergeot is quite near to La Planchoterrie

In 1810 a Joseph Derrieux, 30, a carpenter living at La Gasnerie was a witness at the baptism of Jeanne Derrieux daughter of Michel Derrieux and his wife Magdalene Poirier

So the members of the Derrieux family were widespread throughout the commune and as many shared the names of François, Michel, René etc. it became very difficult to establish the exact family line. However the further I went back so the name of Guy or Gui kept cropping up. Guy born in 1745; another Guy lived from 1712 to 1749, another born in 1630 and another who died in 1640. I began to feel there must be some link with Guy de Rieux, a nobleman from Brittany and a René de Rieux, Lord of Sourdeac born in 1558 who died in 1628; possibly there might even be a link with Jean de Rieux, Lord of Rieux. You can see how 'de Rieux' became 'Derrieux'.

But to go back now to find something more specific and definite about La Vesquerie I went to the library in Gorron where the librarian was very helpful and photocopied for me the pages relevant to La Vesquerie in the Diaries of l'Abbé Angot.

Alphonse-Victor Angot, known as l'Abbé Angot was a French historian specialising in the history of the Mayenne department. He was born in 1844 and died in 1917. He was ordained priest in 1868 in Laval.

From his diaries we find that there was a chapel at La Vesquerie founded before 1598. Please note again the various spellings I have found that were used for La Vequerie, La Vesquerie and La Vacquerie. L'Abbé Angot says that this chapel was founded by Pierre Pouchard and there was one mass a week.

He noted that Brecé was so small in 1686 that the priest wrote to his bishop saying that he was not able to establish a school there as it consisted of only three houses next to the church and they were the presbytery, the manor house and a 'hôtellerie', a hotel business. That sounds a bit grand for such a small place so it must have been what in England at the same time we might have called a coaching inn for travellers. He also said just one very old road traversed the parish going from Chatillon to Gorron and linking to the route to Saint Mars and Ambrières.

It seems that the first school was founded at La Fontaine and there was a combining of some sort with the remains of the chapel at La Vesquerie which possibly had become a school room. A hundred years after the chapel was founded no descendants of Pierre Pouchard could be found to continue paying for the priest so it ceased to be a chapel.

The first maps I came across of this area were the Cassini maps. Giovanni Domenico Cassini, 1625-1712 was the first member of his family to begin work on producing a topographic map of France. He moved to France from Italy and for forty-one years served as astronomer/astrologer to King Louis the fourteenth, the Sun King. Four generations of the Cassini family surveyed France and produced these maps.

During that time some of the surveyors faced great danger as in remote rural areas of the country the inhabitants were not used to seeing strangers and were highly suspicious of a man carrying surveying instruments. This could be witchcraft they thought and sometimes the surveyors were attacked and at least one was killed. At that time France was not a coherent political or cultural entity. Different areas or 'pays' spoke completely different languages and that didn't change much until the speedy travel of the railway age reduced the apparent size and remoteness of the different regions of France.

There on the Cassini map produced in the 1700s is Le Vequerie along with La Fontaine and Les Pins, now known as Le Haut Pin and Le Bas Pin where we know François Derrieux, 1710-1769 and his wife Marie Buas, b1720, lived as later did other members of the Derrieux family. I wonder what they thought about the Cassini surveyors when they came to this area.

The Mongraphie Communale written by the local school master or mistress in 1899 tells us that there was no trace then of the chapel founded by Pierre Pouchard sometime before 1586, possibly at the end of the 1400s when he had bequeathed money for one mass a week. As the Mongraphie says it seems that by 1598 problems arose because no-one could be found to continue paying for the chapel. The priest suggested that the building should be used as a school for boys and it was agreed by the 'grand vicaire' that this should happen with the school master saying prayers every Saturday. Eventually in 1686 this little school was united with a school that had been opened at La Fontaine. Then in 1781 the inhabitants of Brecé decided to have a new school and at the same time the priest, Monsieur Mariel, showed his zeal for girls' education by promising at his own expense to construct a school for girls just like the boys' school and run by the Sisters of Evron.

It was interesting to read about the connection with Evron because we had been there to see the Benedictine Abbey of Notre Dame which was founded in the seventh century. The Abbey there today dates from the eighteenth century.

When we bought the cottage we soon became aware of how difficult it was to understand some of the local people because of their pronounced patois so I was amused to find the following remarks in the Mongraphie Communale written in 1899 by the local school teacher;-

*'Le patois de Brecé est lourd et désagréable, on emploi beaucoup d'expression grossières.'* – 'The patois of Brecé is heavy and disagreeable. Many crude expressions are used.'

After spending some time researching the past I often find myself picturing these people as they went about their daily lives. Lives which were very hard and where life itself was often held by a fragile thread, where poverty, hunger, illness and death were close companions, where they often stayed in bed in the winter when possible; as I have read elsewhere, life was so miserable that 'they lived to die'.

\*\*\*\*\*\*\*\*\*\*\*\*\*

# Bon Appétit
## Leek and Potato Soup

So I feel at the end of that chapter I should do a good peasant style soup.

I cut off the roots and the very coarse green from the top of two leeks and that goes in the compost bin so it goes back to nourish the soil in the potager eventually. Then I cut the next section of green off and wrap the remainder in a plastic bag and put it in the fridge to use another day, but very soon so that they are still fresh when they are used. I half fill my large pan with water and put it on the gas, which is bottled gas here in rural France. I halve the leeks and wash them thoroughly as this is not leek and grit soup. Then I chop them roughly and add them to the pan with chopped unpeeled potatoes, a chopped onion and lots of garlic. Yes lots of garlic, it's good for you as are onions and leeks. I crumble in a chicken stock cube, some salt would do just as well and I add some pepper. I cook it all until the vegetables are tender and then put it to one side to cool before putting it in the liquidiser. It's nearly ready now apart from being reheated. It is fine as it is but I often add some milk or perhaps a little crème fraiche could be stirred in. Delicious.

# Chapter Twelve
## Christmas 2014

We had often had the idea that it would be fun to spend a Christmas at the cottage and with the family otherwise occupied this year it was the perfect time to enjoy a Christmas in France.

On a Saturday ten days before Christmas we noticed that there was a window of calm sea in an otherwise stormy week. The cases were almost packed and just after breakfast we made a snap decision to go that day. The ferry and a cabin were booked, the packing was rapidly finished, the sandwiches prepared for a picnic tea on the boat. After a hurried lunch we were on our way to Portsmouth.

There were only about fifty cars waiting to board plus the usual lorries and once on board it seemed strange that the public areas were so quiet in contrast to the crossings we made in the summer. It was a lovely sunny afternoon, although quite chilly, and we stayed on deck for a while as we glided past the Spinnaker Tower, Nelson's flagship 'Victory' and several of the grey warships which were in port. As the ship moved out into the Solent we saw the settlements nestling into the rolling hills on the Isle of Wight on one side and people enjoying an afternoon stroll on Southsea Common on the other. And up on the sky line behind Portsmouth there was the silhouette of the mock up warship on Portsdown Hill. Further over to the east were the hills of the South Downs with Kingley Vale and the Trundle where we often walk Trixie, who remains tucked up and probably asleep in the car for the crossing.

After a walk around the boat we went back to our west facing cabin and watched as the sun gradually sank towards the horizon producing a golden pathway on the rippling waves stretching out towards the boat. And then it was gone and a cold winter's night was upon us but we were warm in our cabin and settled down for a sleep.

Later, as the flashes from a lighthouse on the Cotentin peninsula signalled that we were approaching the coast of France we ate our sandwiches and had a small glass of wine each.

We needed our wits about us for the two hour drive to the cottage through the dark, first round the Caen périphérique, usually so busy when we get the morning ferry and arrive in the afternoon but now in the late evening much quieter, then off down the dual carriageway to Falaise before setting off across country to Putanges Pont Ecrepin situated beside the River Orne, so pretty in the summer but now silent and deserted on this cold night.

The car thermometer showed -1°C then -3°C and from time to time we became engulfed in patches of swirling fog. A few of the villages we passed through had coloured lights hanging across the road; in one place they wished us 'Bon Fêtes' but mostly this late at night there were few lights showing and it was a dark world. As the miles sped by and we drove through the familiar places of Lassey les Chateaux and Ambrières we were anticipating the imminent end of our journey.

Finally just before midnight we reached the cottage and turned into the drive we shared with our neighbours; all was quiet and their lights were out. We climbed out of the car into the freezing night stretching our travel weary limbs. As I held the torch John struggled with the padlock and bolt on the outer wooden shutter and then opened the inner door and at last we were back in our small stone cottage in France.

First the electricity had to be turned on. What a difference it makes when everything is illuminated! The priority for me was to get the electric blankets plugged in to start warming up the cold beds so I went upstairs to do that and had a quick check round to see that all was well which it was apart from a few of last autumn's dead flies lying around. Thinking ahead we had put on the winter duvets and left the electric blankets ready in the beds when we had departed for home in October.

The next priority was lighting the wood burner and it was a cheering sight to see the wood catching alight and after only a few minutes to feel some warmth coming from the fire.

As expected it was very cold, 8C inside, but

once we had unpacked the car the cottage had started to warm up a little. John had turned the water on so now the small water tank started heating up and the electric towel rail in the bathroom started very slowly to emit warmth. In the winter it takes a whole day for the cottage to become completely cosy.

When we had unpacked the car and put most things away we sat in front of the fire with a glass of wine while the beds warmed up. Despite that it was so cold that I slept in my fleecy dressing gown over my pyjamas that first night.

Trixie was wearing her emerald green pyjamas to keep her warm but she came upstairs in the night squeaking as she does when she wants something. Having been woken up by her John went down to replenish the fire with logs and he brought her new bed upstairs. We had brought a thick winter duvet from home for her and folded double it made a lovely cosy bed. She came up squeaking on a few subsequent nights but we took no notice of her and she soon decided to return to her comfy bed which had been left downstairs after the first night.

The next morning was bright and frosty. Everywhere looked so pretty with thick rime on the tall grasses that remained from the summer in the flower bed near the cottage. The landscape shone and sparkled so we decided to walk down to the river while the sun was shining. Unfortunately with La Chasse popping off their guns somewhere on the other side of the valley Trixie was reluctant to go anywhere. 'They were out to get her,' she said, 'It wasn't safe; whatever were we thinking of?'

But it was such a beautiful morning and we enjoyed the walk anyway. Last time we were here the maize harvest had just finished and now some of the fields were already green, planted with winter wheat or a green manure crop. The trees, still in leaf when we went home in October, were now bare silhouettes against a blue sky. A buzzard flew overhead plaintively mewing as it looked for small rodents to eat. We went down the track past La Closerie where we noticed a bit more of the roof had collapsed. And then down the hill to the river which was high and swirling noisily under the bridge after recent rain. Water was even flowing through the mill race. On our way back we observed the trees that had held walnuts and medlars in the autumn were now stripped bare. The time when the land was yielding its harvest was over and now larder shelves were well stocked for the cold months ahead.

Later John was outside when our neighbour, just setting off for his twelve kilometre Sunday morning run stopped to proudly announce, "Je suis grandpère!" We had known that his son's wife had been expecting an addition to the family and now here was one very proud grandfather who knew all the details about the length and weight of the baby boy who was just a month old.

The next day we went to Super U where our neighbour's wife works. When we congratulated her she asked how old our grandchildren were and on hearing that they were twenty-four, nineteen and sixteen decided we might be 'grandparent-arrières' before long. Goodness me, great grandparents; the very idea makes me feel old.

On these cold dark mornings before Christmas it's very tempting to snuggle down under my warm duvet and defer the act of getting up. As I mentioned in the last chapter the peasants in these country areas did just that and stayed in bed in the winter, a sort of semi-hibernation I suppose. That saved on fuel and food but when they did have to get up their homes must have been frightfully cold. However they frequently shared them with their animals each giving the other warmth. And they shared the ripe smell too!

I was amused to see in Super U that those long sausage like draught excluders for putting at the base of doors were being sold. There you can buy your 'bas de porte' for 6.90€ each. I haven't seen those in England since I was a child.

At the end of the week we went to the special Christmas lunch at Le Briccius in the village. I've already mentioned this restaurant elsewhere and the warm welcome we are given. This particular occasion was no exception and I was interested to see that the usual workmen who go there every day for their lunch were also there for this Christmas meal. Apparently the firms they work for pay for their everyday lunches as part of their wages and that included today's festive spread. The cost of the normal lunch has now gone up to twelve euros and this Christmas lunch was sixteen euros. For that we had a glass of kir to start with and there was white wine going round too, then either a sort of Coquille St Jacques in a vol au vent or a warm paté en croute. After that there was steak or duck. We both chose duck and it was served with a large half tomato cooked with some pesto on the top and also a sort of small potato pancake. After that there was lettuce, with the usual delicious dressing and two types of cheese, then a fruit tarte followed by an orange, a chocolate and coffee.

The workmen, usually so quiet, were certainly in the festive spirit and there was a lot of laughter. It was very busy and it had been decided to have two sittings so that everybody who wanted to eat there that day could be accommodated. We went to the first one at midday and the second was due at half past one but by one forty five the first sitting had not finished. The waitresses were really under pressure and were rushing around with several plates on one arm and after a course had been finished had to carry huge stacks of plates to the kitchen.

One of the waitresses really amused us as she did everything at a run including carrying stacks of plates and then hurling herself bottom first at the swing door into the kitchen. For another young waitress who had been drafted in to help it was probably her first time there and she seemed unsure of what to do. It was a baptism of fire for her to be there for the first time on such a busy day. Unlike the girl who did everything at a run she had difficulty in opening the heavy swing door into the kitchen and we felt sorry for her each time she struggled to pass through.

So with the first sitting finishing late the next batch of diners were beginning to gather for the second sitting. We were amazed when they came in and started to help clear the tables, shaking the cloths and setting their own places. It was all very good humoured.

Although the weather was misty most of the time we were at the cottage and there were some rainy days too, there was enough dry weather for us to get some essential jobs done in the garden. John mowed the grass which was rather shaggy; had it been left until March it would have been very unkempt. I weeded the long border and was glad to be able to remove some deep rooted buttercups and dandelions which would have been very difficult to get rid of in March when the one hundred tulips that

John had planted in October would already be above ground. Yes we are already thinking ahead to our next visit in the spring when the daffodils will be in flower and the birds will be singing.

Christmas arrived and we put up a little silver tree and hung our Christmas cards over the window. Martin and Gina came over for a glass of fizz and we went to them the evening before we came home. We went to other friends for a coffee, a mince pie and a slice of Bûche de Noel one morning and we listened to the carols, old and new from Kings College Chapel at Cambridge on Christmas Eve. The atmosphere for Christmas was now just right. Here in this small cottage on this quiet lane in France all was peaceful while elsewhere the final Christmas preparations were drawing to a climax.

I remember when I was teaching how the excitement used to build as the end of the Christmas term approached. It was a generally sticky time with the making of decorations and with the class parties but then there was the nativity play, the same story re-enacted each year by small children, the sweet story of the first Christmas. And if it should snow these children would gravitate to the classroom window to see the magical snowflakes gently drifting down.

For us in France Christmas morning dawned, pleasantly sunny for a change. After opening our presents we walked with Trixie down by the river. It was so peaceful with the river flowing gently on its way and the sunbeams filtering through the trees.

In an animal trap near the river bank a coypu was powerless in a cage and I thought of prisoners the world over on this Christmas morning denied their freedom for whatever reason.

Thankful for our freedom we returned home and phoned our families in England. Tim and Sue's daughter, away from home at Christmas for the first time, was having a wonderful time being a chalet maid at an Italian ski resort where she would be skiing for most of Christmas Day before resuming her more onerous duties in the late afternoon.

A few days later it was time for us to leave. It was very cold overnight and as we left at about 10am the sun was rising and shining on the icy roads. There had been a light dusting of snow and the pine trees in the forest near Carrouges were sparkling under a lacy mantle. Rather than go on the boat to Portsmouth we had decided to drive to Calais and go through Le Tunnel sous La Manche. It was a clear frosty day; a beautiful day to be driving through the French countryside. It was busy at the tunnel with skiers and other holiday makers returning to the UK. Later that evening we arrived home in Chichester safely and so concluded our visits to France for another year.

\*\*\*\*\*\*\*\*\*\*\*\*

*Le Briccius, Brecé*

# Bon Appétit
## Tarte Fine Tomate et Pesto

This recipe uses two packets of ready rolled puff pastry.

Eight tomatoes

A jar of pesto

Fresh basil.

Cut each sheet of pastry into four rectangles and fork over the central part where the filling will go. Place onto baking parchment.

On each piece of pastry place a spoonful of pesto leaving a margin round the edge.

On top of the pesto place slices of tomato.

Bake for twenty minutes at 180°C.

Decorate with a sprig of fresh basil and serve hot or cold with a salad.

# Conclusion

All the hard work on the cottage and in the garden have brought us great enjoyment and it has truly become our home in France. The beauty of this area, the people and its history have gained a place in our hearts.

The years seem to pass more and more quickly as time goes on. Each one now is precious and as we are getting older we know that our years here will be limited but we are going to enjoy our time to the full. So if you are walking along the lane on your way to the river and you see us sitting in the garden with a glass of wine give a friendly wave and call out 'Bonjour' and we will wish you 'Bon route'.

But for now it is 'Au revoir'.

*This is my favourite photo of the garden*

All the photos in this book can be seen in full colour on Susie's web site.

http://www.susiewilliams.coffeecup.com

Printed in Great Britain
by Amazon